Engaging Learners through Zoom is like a banquet of ideas for polls, chats, breakout rooms, using the main session as a central hub, and far more. What's terrific about this book is that it gives concrete, innovative examples for practically every discipline—any instructor can benefit! I never knew I needed this book, but now, I couldn't do without it!

—Dr. Barbara Oakley, Coursera "Innovation Instructor" of the world's most popular MOOC; Ramón y Cajal Distinguished Scholar of Global Digital Learning, McMaster University; Engineering Professor, Oakland University, and author of *A Mind for Numbers*, *Learning How to Learn*, and *Mindshift*.

In this amazing resource, Dr. Brennan examines all the Zoom course delivery tools—polls, chats, breakout rooms, whiteboards, integrated apps, and so on. For each tool, he outlines a broad variety of learning structures (10 for polls alone), with numerous examples in different disciplines. His engaging writing style gives you the impression that you're sitting with a knowledgeable and friendly colleague who can help you do anything with Zoom you want to do, and deal with any problem that may arise. An indispensable "how-to" book in a field is often dubbed the bible of that field. I am certain that this book will quickly become the bible for Zoom users, and possibly for all online instructors.

—Dr. Richard Felder, Hoechst Celanese Professor Emeritus of Chemical Engineering, North Carolina State University; coauthor of *Teaching and Learning STEM: A Practical Guide* and *Elementary Principles of Chemical Processes*.

Dr. Brennan has insightfully applied principles from the learning sciences, motivation research, On Course, and emotional intelligence to demonstrate how Zoom sessions can be fun and exciting for instructors as well as students. While this book is invaluable for instructors teaching remotely, it is also vital for face-to-face teaching because of the treasure trove of examples, from a multitude of disciplines, that are applicable to both environments.

—Dr. Saundra Yancy McGuire, author, *Teach Students How to Learn*; Director Emerita, Center for Academic Success; (Ret) Assistant Vice Chancellor and Professor of Chemistry, Louisiana State University

Faculty have been waiting for this book! *Engaging Learners through Zoom* is filled with practical strategies (and clear, detailed directions) that educators at any level can use to engage students in online classes. The book also offers multiple research-based strategies to address physical, cognitive, and emotional Zoom fatigue.

—Dr. Teresa Ward, Professional Development Faculty Coordinator, Butte College

As someone who has had to quickly master a variety of new, online tools, reading this book felt like having an experienced, supportive mentor at my fingertips. *Engaging Learners through Zoom* offers a wealth of innovative solutions for many of the challenges confronting student-centered educators who now find themselves in online classrooms. Grounded in research on learning, this practical guide translates best practices in student engagement into strategies that can be implemented in my teaching right away. It provides concise, well-designed activities in a variety of disciplines and step-by-step guidance for implementing them with online tools.

—Dr. Kristie Daniel-DiGregorio, Professor,
Human Development, El Camino College

This book is a must-have and will change how you view and teach online with Zoom. The level of detail is thoughtful, providing examples for various subjects with attention paid to diversity and inclusion, and it has a "preventing issues and troubleshooting" section in each chapter. There are so many ideas—my favorites are the "Obstacle Race" and "Dance Party."

—Dr. Lea Beth Lewis, Assistant Director (Emeriti),
The University Learning Center, California State University, Fullerton

As students transition to the virtual world, faculty are finding Zoom an exhausting and unfulfilling prospect. Lacking the tools to engage students in the synchronous environment, they are getting tired of searching for instructional suggestions on the Web. Dr. Brennan's book to the rescue. It's easy to use this book as an essential guide that will ensure greater learning for students and less fatigue for instructors.

—Michelle Francis, Professional Development
Coordinator, West Valley College

There is no better educator, researcher, and overall student success champion than Dr. Jonathan Brennan to share his years of wisdom in the classroom (and now on Zoom). Dr. Brennan weaves his mastery and passion for engaging college students into the virtual world with this outstanding book that could not be more timely.

—Andrea Shaw, Assistant Dean, Marketing and Communication, Santa
Clara University Leavey School of Business

Professor Brennan's strategies are immediately attractive to anyone striving to engage students. The book's explanations and directions are simple and practical, and easy to imagine and implement. This collection is a very welcome resource in this challenging time. Within 10 minutes of starting through the book, I had several apps open and was upping my game for classes and meetings alike!

—Chris Weidenbach, English Department Chair,
Professional Development Committee, Laney College

The world has turned upside down, and ready or not, we're all online. Now what? Dr. Brennan's oh-so-timely offering provides the step-by-step answer to that question. It's a gift to faculty longing to keep students and active learning at the heart of instruction, even in a Zoom-centric world.

—Katie O'Brien, EOPS Counselor/Professor,
Staff Development Coordinator, Rio Hondo College

Brennan's guide to active learning on Zoom will be useful as our colleagues around the nation (and the world) seek to better leverage tech tools to make the online environment active and virtual interactions more genuine. He is dedicated to student success and is extraordinarily skilled as a facilitator.

—William Patrick Barlow, Emeritus Faculty/Director of the Center for
Excellence in Teaching and Learning, Madison College

If you are an online educator in any discipline, you absolutely NEED this book; it's phenomenal! Keeping our students engaged is now more critical than ever, and this book delivers. It provides educators with step-by-step instructions to effectively utilize Zoom to promote learning and minimize Zoom fatigue. Using this book, I have seen a significant increase in student participation and engagement, which gives me hope.

—Ann Brandon, English/Reading Instructor and Professional Development
Coordinator, Clovis Community College

Engaging Learners through Zoom

Strategies for virtual teaching across disciplines

JONATHAN BRENNAN

Jossey-Bass A Wiley Imprint 111 River Street, Hoboken NJ 07030—www.josseybass.com

Jossey-Bass books and products are available through most bookstores. To contact Jossey-Bass directly, call our Customer Care Department within the U.S. at 800–956–7739, outside the U.S. at +1 317 572 3986, or fax +1 317 572 4002.

Wiley also publishes its books in a variety of electronic formats and by print-on-demand. Some material included with standard print versions of this book may not be included in e-books or in print-on-demand. If this book refers to media such as a CD or DVD that is not included in the version you purchased, you may download this material at http://booksupport.wiley.com. For more information about Wiley products, visit www.wiley.com.

Library of Congress Cataloging-in-Publication Data is Available:

ISBN 9781119783145 (paperback)
ISBN 9781119783176 (ePDF)
ISBN 9781119783152 (epub)

Cover Design: Wiley
Cover Images: (background) © NeMaria/Shutterstock, (inset) © Natalya Novella/Shutterstock, On Course Logo Courtesy of On Course Inc

Printed in the United States of America

first edition SKY10021185_091420

This book is dedicated to the ones I love, and with deep gratitude to the Honorable John Lewis, who has crossed his final bridge.

Contents

Acknowledgments

I'd like to extend my appreciation to a remarkable group of educators, the On Course Facilitator team: Robin Middleton, Deb Poese, Eileen Zamora, Mark McBride, LuAnn Wood, Amy Pawlik, and Chris Strouthopoulos. I appreciate your dedication, support, wisdom, and humor. I honor your determination and many contributions to our students and colleagues in higher education. In the midst of challenging times, you make it all worthwhile.

I'd also like to thank the nearly 2,000 On Course Ambassadors, whose volunteer efforts are helping to transform the lives of students across North America (and the world). Thanks as well to the more than 50,000 educators who have attended On Course professional development events. Your creativity and persistence are an outstanding model for your students.

Special thanks to Deb Poese, Robin Middleton, and Carolina Williams for their thoughtful and careful feedback on the manuscript.

A big thanks to songwriter John Prine for an inspiring life playlist. Hello in there.

About the Author

Dr. Jonathan Brennan is a faculty member in the English Department at Mission College in Santa Clara, California. He is a researcher in best practices in student success, holds a BA and an MA in English (UC Berkeley), an MA in Counseling Psychology (USM), a PhD in Comparative Ethnic Studies (UC Berkeley), and an EdD in Leadership and Change (Fielding University). He has chaired the Student Success Committee, English Department and Language Arts Division, and served as VP of the Academic Senate and on multiple distance-learning committees.

He was voted Faculty of the Year at Mission College and awarded a NISOD Teaching Excellence Award in 2000. In 2005, he was awarded the Stanback-Stroud Diversity award from the California State Academic Senate and in 2008 the California State Hayward Award for Excellence in Education. Since 2006, he has been Chair of the On Course National Conference and is currently editor of the *On Course Student Success Newsletter*, which has nearly 150,000 subscribers worldwide. He has facilitated workshops on improving student engagement and learning for over 6,000 faculty from colleges and universities across North America.

Dr. Brennan's other books include *On Course: Strategies for Success in College, Career, and Life* (Cengage), *Choosing a Good Road* (a student success textbook for high school students), *Mixed Race Literature* (Stanford Press), and *When Br'er Rabbit Meets Coyote*: *African–Native American Literature* (University of Illinois Press). In the last two decades, he has focused his research on higher education leadership; best practices in noncognitive learner competencies; effectiveness in distance learning; and the intersection between race, culture, equity, and access to education.

Dr. Brennan has been teaching online courses since 2003 and was a member of the Academic Senate Committee on Distance Learning. He has taught using multiple content management system platforms, including ETUDES, Blackboard, Angel, and Canvas. He has assessed online courses for the demonstration of regular, effective student contact and engaged learning. He developed the On Course Online workshop and is the lead designer of the new, engaging On Course Zoom workshops.

On Course workshops (www.oncourseworkshop.com) offer educators the opportunity to acquire new best practices in both supporting online learners in strengthening noncognitive variables and in designing and implementing active online learning structures that improve learning outcomes, success rates, and retention.

Dr. Brennan has also presented on African–Native American Literature and Black Indian Subjectivity at the Modern Language Association and American Literature Association meetings, and published articles in the *African American National Biography, A/B: Auto/Biography Studies* and *Oxford Companion to African American Literature*. He has written five musicals, including adaptations of Mark Twain's *Pudd'nhead Wilson*, Harriet Jacobs's *Incidents in the Life of a Slave Girl*, and Washington Irving's *Legend of Sleepy Hollow*.

Introduction: Zoom and Active Learning Structures

Though the use of distance learning has been a steadily growing trend in education, due to the Covid-19 pandemic, educators in 2020 made a dramatic shift from in-person classrooms to virtual learning platforms like Zoom, Google Meet, and Microsoft Teams, among others. Some educators have been excited about the new learning opportunities, but many have experienced overwhelm, frustration, and mixed results in promoting student engagement and learning.

Like our students, many educators have experienced "Zoom fatigue" from both distance meetings and teaching; thus, we have some understanding of our students' experiences. Many educators are frustrated with the perceived limitations of video conferencing platforms like Zoom that were originally designed for corporate meetings. Yet Zoom and other platforms offer tools that, with a little creativity and practice, can be used to more deeply engage students, reduce Zoom Fatigue, promote active learning and achieve successful learning outcomes.

This book is a collection of dozens of active, synchronous online learning structures that can be used in any discipline, on multiple video conferencing platforms, and at multiple levels of education, K-12 through higher education. Over 150 strategies with step-by-step directions are offered across more than 83 disciplines, with multiple examples for 26 of the most commonly taught courses.

Active learning structures backed by cognitive neuroscience are exactly what my organization, On Course, has been offering to educators for decades. I am excited by the opportunity to share the innovative best practices On Course has developed to more fully engage learners. My goal for this book is to provide you with a toolbox for improving distance learning experiences and outcomes. If you use these tools with students, On Course will achieve its organizational goal of significantly increasing learner engagement, and thus the opportunity for more students to achieve their educational and life goals. Your students will be easier to work with, and you'll probably have more fun!

We'd appreciate your feedback on both these strategies and the existing Zoom platform, and ways they might be enhanced with additional features directly relevant to distance education. We'd also love to collect new success strategies to offer educators. Please contact us: www.oncourseworkshop.com.

It's a time of great change for us all. I hope you will collaborate with your colleagues and students to optimize Zoom and produce lasting, positive change in education, both for hybrid and distance learning.

Polls

POLLS

Polls are one of the best features of Zoom, and they provide an opportunity for instructors and students to receive real-time feedback. Polls support the introduction, clarification, and reinforcement of concepts introduced in the learning sessions. There are numerous ways to use polls in your Zoom meetings. They can be used as an opening to a learning session, periodically throughout the session, or as a closing poll to set up the next assignment or class meeting. Polls can be developed and loaded beforehand for a classroom meeting or created on the spot when an essential question occurs to an instructor. Polls can be conducted anonymously or share participant information.

Account Settings

In your Zoom account, under Settings, then the Meeting tab, select the In-Meeting (Basic) controls. Locate and enable "Polling: Add 'Polls' to the meeting controls."

If you want to create polls in advance, schedule the meeting, then click to view the meeting details. Note the space at the bottom for meeting polls, and use the Add feature to make a new poll.

Each question can be built to be single choice (participants can select only one answer) or multiple choice (participants can select multiple answers). You can create up to 25 polls total including both before and during meetings.

If you are using a meeting template with existing polls, you can edit those polls at this time also. (NOTE: If you have created recurring meetings, the polls are built for all meetings at once.)

Meeting Controls

The Poll control button is located at the bottom center of the Zoom window. If you did not choose to build any polls in advance, you will see an option to add a question and will be taken to the poll creation window in your Zoom account. If you have existing polls built, you will see an arrow to open a pull-down list and select the desired poll, or you can select Edit to create a new poll on the spot. Use "Launch Poll" to get your question(s) out to the participants.

Once you end the poll, select Share Results if you wish to show and discuss the results with attendees. You can also download a polling report after the meeting.

---

1. Icebreaker Polls

An instructor can use Icebreaker Polls to create community at the start of a term. They can focus on personal background, student roles, academic topics, or fun topics that are light and easy to answer. Instructors can use a quick, single-question poll at the start of the first session to offer each individual student an opportunity to develop an answer. After a couple minutes, students can be paired or placed in small groups to share their responses using Breakout Rooms or Chat.

> **Student Role:** Which one of the following do you expect to be your biggest challenge in succeeding at college this semester? 1) Managing procrastination, 2) Paying for tuition and textbooks, 3) Handling online classes, 4) Dealing with family and friend issues, or 5) Studying effectively for tests.

> **Academic Topic:** Which of these statements do you believe to be true about **Quantum Physics**?

1. Quantum physics is all about uncertainty.
2. Almost nobody actually understands quantum physics.
3. Quantum physics has led to numerous inventions of practical tools.
4. The analogy of Schrödinger's cat is useful in understanding quantum physics.

Fun Topic: If you were a vegetable, which of the following vegetables would you be, and why? 1) Broccoli, 2) Kale, 3) Snow Pea, 4) Cabbage, 5) Spinach, or 6) Green Bean.

2. Starter Polls

A Starter Poll can be offered right at the start of the session to immediately engage learners in a topic, connect learners to the rest of the group, or to provide important information to the instructor about the cohort of learners, their mindset/attitude, or learning needs. Starter polls can draw from elements of any of the other poll types, such as a prediction poll to spark learner curiosity before being introduced to the topics or a reflection poll to process content from a prior class meeting or homework assignment. Starter polls can assume some prior knowledge from reading or class discussion, or ask about topics which have yet to be introduced (though topics or concepts may be defined if needed to provide students some basic information and context for their answer).

Civil Engineering: Which one of the four concrete tests addressed in the textbook reading needs further explanation? 1) Air content, 2) Slump, 3) Compression cylinder, or 4) Flexural beam.

Abnormal Psychology: Which condition do you think is most common among the general population in the United States? 1) Phobia, 2) Panic Disorder, 3) Obsessive Compulsive Disorder, 4) Generalized Anxiety Disorder, or 5) Post-Traumatic Stress Disorder.

Sociology: Which of these two elements, *Role Strain* or *Role Conflict*, presents a greater challenge to your ability to be an effective student in this course? [*Role Strain* can create overwhelm in managing multiple tasks associated with various student roles: testing, attending class, studying, for example. *Role Conflict* can create overwhelm when negotiating life roles such as parent, employee, friend, roommate, and so forth.]

3. Prediction Polls

These Polls ask participants to make a prediction about data, rules, outcomes, or future events. By asking students to predict the possible outcome of an event or experiment, students become more quickly engaged in the material, triggering their innate curiosity. Predictions can be about drawing reasonable conclusions from known facts or predicting unknown results based on prior learning.

Prediction polls ask learners to look for clues, teaching them to be more careful readers and observers. They also invite critical thinking and analysis. Even guessing (if not completely random) on the part of learners can be useful, if you circle back around to ask them to explain the basis of their prediction. Students can be asked to make viable predictions, and this can be directed by the pool of potential answers in a prediction poll. Pre-instruction questions have been shown to increase subsequent retention of concepts by about 10%, even if the learners were unable to initially identify the correct answer (Little & Bjork, 2011).

After a poll is closed, responders' predictions can be addressed immediately or can be confirmed through careful attention when the material is introduced. Their predictions can be revised or corrected when presented with actual evidence.

> **World History:** Considering both past pandemic migrations, and your prediction of the impact on world migration patterns from the Covid-19 pandemic, what percentage of the population might be displaced from their current locations? (8%, 12%, 15%, 18%, or 23%)
>
> **Physics:** Based on what you have just learned about **Newton's First Law of Motion** (An object at rest remains at rest, or if in motion, remains in motion at a constant velocity unless acted on by a net external force), which of the following do you believe **Newton's Second Law of Motion** might be, and why is it the second law?
>
> 1. For every action (force) in nature there is an equal and opposite reaction.
> 2. The acceleration of an object is dependent upon two variables—the net force acting upon the object and the mass of the object.
>
> **English:** Which one of these three writing errors will be the most frequent error on the next sets of student essays, and why? 1) Sentence Fragments, 2) Sentence Run-ons, or 3) Comma Splices.

4. Reflection Polls

Try a Reflection Poll when you want to offer learners an opportunity to consider implications, connections, and application of concepts to which they have just been introduced. Periodic reflection is an essential part of the learning process (Chang, B., 2019). It clarifies learner comprehension, creates an opportunity to generate questions, and promotes contextualization, offering a framework for new knowledge.

Biology: Which steps of the Gram stain procedures are most clear to you (Poll 1), and which steps need more explanation (Poll 2)?

1. Applying a primary stain (crystal violet) to a heat-fixed smear of a bacterial culture
2. The addition of iodide, which binds to crystal violet and traps it in the cell
3. Rapid decolorization with ethanol or acetone
4. Counterstaining with safranin

Mathematics: Which of the three methods of solving quadratic equations (Factoring, Completing the Square, or Quadratic Formula) do you use most confidently? Why do you think you prefer this method over the other two?

Political Science: Which one legislative or judicial outcome resulting from the various campaigns of the Civil Rights Movement(s) has created the greatest impact on your own life?

1. Civil Rights Act (1964)
2. Voting Rights Act (1965)
3. *Loving v. Virginia* (case ending anti-miscegenation laws) (1967)
4. Fair Housing Act (1968)

5. Engagement Polls

The Engagement Poll offers the instructor an opportunity to check the level of learner connection to the current topic or activity (or to themselves). Research has shown that learner engagement is a strong indicator for predicting learning performance (*Student Engagement*, Stanford Center for Opportunity Policy in Education, 2016). An Engagement Poll can be very specific to course topics or focus more on learner attitude and experience. Four elements of engagement that might be assessed include relevance, autonomy, collaboration, and authenticity.

The instructor can determine whether to continue an activity, modify it to increase engagement, or introduce a different activity that might help students become more interested in the topic, renewing learner focus.

Course Topic Engagement Polls might include the following questions (**Accounting**):

- What is your level of interest in learning more about the Balance Sheet? (1–10).
- Rank the level of value to you of learning to complete Adjusted Journal Entries (1–10).
- Score your level of motivation to continue today's lesson on Cost-Benefit Analysis (1–10).
- Which of the following six topics is most interesting to you? (Accounting Standards, Assets Auditing, Bank Reconciliations, Bankruptcy, Billing, Bookkeeping) Which is the least interesting to you?

Learner Attitude/Experience Engagement Polls might include the following questions:

- Rate the amount of attention you are giving this session's topic (1–10).
- Are you currently multitasking (be honest; this poll is anonymous!) on other tabs/screens (Y/N)?
- Rank your learning attitude for this class session, from 1—very unwilling to learn something new, to 10—very open to learning something new.

6. Survey Polls

Using Survey Polls helps the instructor gather information about student behavior, tasks, and experiences that can help the instructor with course planning and assignments, as well as identifying needed learning support and resources.

Business: How many sources have you identified for your Social Entrepreneurship research project? (1, 2, 3, 4, or 5+)

Nursing: Rank the level of effectiveness of your Triage Study Team during its weekly review meeting (1—very ineffective to 10—very effective).

Music: Which source did you find most useful in understanding the development of the genre of Trip-Hop (Downtempo)? 1) Chapter Three textbook description, 2) the Interview with DJ Milo, or 3) listening to *The Wild Bunch* playlist.

7. Gallery Polls

These polls are used to rank a display of instructor- or student-generated materials that can be evaluated in a virtual "Gallery Walk." Imagine walking through an art gallery to view images and sculptures. A face-to-face Gallery

Walk provides an opportunity to individual or grouped learners to generate a learning artifact (like an idea poster or design model specific to the course discipline) that is displayed by posting on a physical wall or set on tables. Students then visit the gallery of ideas to rank, critique, ask questions, and engage with the class ideas, often moderated by the instructor. A virtual display can be achieved by using Padlet (see Chapter 8) or another app, or through the Share Screen option in Zoom.

When the materials generated are text, they can be inserted by the instructor as poll answer options, then run as a poll to elicit learner opinions. If the materials are images, they can be posted as numbered images (on Padlet, for example) or in a Google Doc, and then the poll can be run to gather opinions.

> **English:** Choose the thesis statement that most closely follows the Criteria for an Effective Thesis.

> **Kinesiology/Physical Education:** Which team display shows the most innovative tool to replace a caliper (which determines composition: fat percentage, and lean body mass including muscle and bone mass)?

> **Communication Studies (Speech):** Which of the posted Narrative Speech Outlines is most likely to result in an effective presentation?

8. Comprehension (Testing) Polls

Comprehension (Testing) Polls allow you to offer basic, ungraded assessments to measure a learner's grasp of essential concepts from current or prior lessons. They can be assigned for individual, paired, team, or whole class testing. Polls are limited in their use for extensive testing and are more often used for practice, surveying, and other ways to increase learner engagement intended to improve subsequent testing and understanding. They allow a focused review of one or several questions. Polls, unlike tests, are more typically conducted anonymously, and they are often shared with participants immediately afterwards. Polls can also be conducted without subsequent sharing to allow an instructor to gather essential information. The Zoom Polls allow single or multiple-choice questions.

Research on Retrieval Practice demonstrates that frequent testing (using various testing/practice methods such as taking quizzes, responding to prompts, and studying with flashcards) promotes long-term learning. The more difficult the assigned task (assuming the learner has background knowledge and tools to solve the problem), the greater the benefit for long-term learning, so this is an opportunity to use some higher-level questions. The intention of retrieval practice through polls is that the practice be short and focused, accomplished within a maximum of 10–15 minutes.

Chemistry:

1. Which bonds are formed from the transfer of electrons (Covalent or Ionic)?
2. Which bonds exist as discrete molecular units (versus arrays or crystals) (Covalent or Ionic compounds)?
3. Which compound is nonflammable: Ionic (inorganic) or Covalent (organic)?

Anthropology: Which branch of anthropology focuses most on a fieldwork approach?

1. Cultural Anthropology
2. Social Anthropology
3. Biological Anthropology
4. Linguistic Anthropology

Forestry Studies: A flank fire has which of the following characteristics?

1. Burns hotter than the average fire
2. Runs with the wind
3. Burns into the wind
4. Burns parallel to the wind
5. Burns cooler than the average fire

Computer Engineering: Which one(s) of the following are part of the six operating system tasks?

1. Processor Management
2. Memory Management
3. Storage Management
4. User Interface
5. System Management
6. Application Interface

Fashion Design: Which of the following refers to the amount of roominess in a garment?

1. Grain Line
2. Dart
3. Tuck
4. Ease

9. Practice Polls

The Practice Poll is a form of Retrieval Practice and can be used for periodic practice of crucial skills. The poll can assign a problem for solo, paired, or team practice with various answer options. As a team, students collaborate to choose an answer selected from the poll options. Poll results can be displayed to share correct and incorrect responses, then concepts and problem-solving approaches can be discussed.

> **Chemical Engineering:** Discuss the following concept with your assigned team and run trial calculations to determine an answer: A chemical reaction will occur spontaneously at constant pressure and temperature if the free energy is:
>
> 1. Zero
> 2. Positive
> 3. Negative
> 4. None of the Above
>
> **English Composition:** Review the paragraph displayed through Share Screen and determine if the primary problem is:
>
> 1. Syntax
> 2. Tone
> 3. Coherence
> 4. Development
>
> **First-Year Experience/Student Success:** With your assigned partner, explore the Case Study emailed to participants and select the poll response option that you think best solves the challenges faced by the student in the case study.

10. Closing Polls

To provide learners an opportunity for a final reflection or to collect feedback on the class session, try a Closing Poll.

1. **Art History:** How much did you learn today about Iconographic Analysis? (1—very little to 10—enough to feel confident about the next test)
2. How valuable do you believe the weekly online office hour to be? (1—not at all valuable to 10—better than the class sessions)
3. What is your level of willingness to ask questions through Chat during the class sessions? (1—very unwilling through 10—very willing and already have)

PREVENTING ISSUES AND TROUBLESHOOTING

Edit Polls

If you click on EDIT POLLS, it doesn't actually allow you to "edit" the current poll. Instead, it opens a new poll that you can create as though you were using the "Add Poll" feature in your Zoom account. If you wish to edit the poll instead of creating a new one, close the new poll window using the top right "X," then click on the poll you wish to edit. You cannot edit the poll after you have already run it during the meeting.

If you want to use the results of a classroom meeting activity to add answers to an existing poll question, or modify the question, create the poll before the meeting, then click Edit Poll (see above) or log into your account to edit the draft poll you have created.

Stop Sharing

Be sure to Stop Sharing the poll after reviewing results with students or if you have decided not to share results after the students have completed the poll. It will not come off the screen unless you stop sharing.

Polls Not Working

If a poll won't run or doesn't appear in the Poll toggle options, Polls may not be activated in meeting settings before the meeting starts. In your Zoom account, under Settings, then the Meeting tab, select the In-Meeting (Basic) controls. Locate and enable "Polling: Add 'Polls' to the meeting controls."

Sometimes there may be a problem with the Poll function if you are using an older operating system on your computer. It's time to upgrade. ☺

Gallery Polls and Using Padlet

If you use Padlet (see Chapter 8) to display Gallery Poll items, be sure to verify that the link you send to the Padlet works to access the site, and that you have chosen the Public Share setting on Padlet for it to be shared with anyone.

REFERENCE

1. Little, Jeri & Bjork, Elizabeth. (2011). *Pretesting with multiple-choice questions facilitates learning.* Conference: Cognitive Science Society.

Chat

CHAT

The Chat feature in Zoom offers endless variations of learning activities. It is likely one of the most overlooked features, as Chat's very simplicity can also obscure more-sophisticated uses. Because the Chat feature can lead to learner distraction if not managed properly, some instructors simply disable users' ability to chat with anyone other than the host or co-host. Once Chat is enabled in your Account Settings for the meeting, you can use the in-meeting controls to change the settings to make strategic use of Chat.

I recommend that the Chat in-meeting default be limited to privately chatting to the host or co-host only, during most of the class meeting. If not, students will sometimes use Chat for "side-talking," which, just like in the physical classroom, can be a distraction both to their own learning as well as others' learning. However, there are many times when you want to leverage the Chat feature to enhance communication opportunities, learning, and social networking.

Why is using Chat so important? Not only does it give you numerous options for engaging students, but it's also a tool that the majority of learners are highly motivated to use. In 2018, people between the ages of 18 and 24 sent 2,022 texts and received 1,831 texts per month. Billions more messages are sent every year through messaging apps like iPhone Messages, Android Messages, WhatsApp, and Facebook Messenger. Both teenagers and adults report that texting/messaging is their preferred method of communication over speaking in person ("How many texts do people send every day?" Kenneth Burke, 2018).

Existing learner proficiency with the use of Chat combined with user enthusiasm offer educators an excellent opportunity to leverage Chat technology for active learning. The more Zoom features we use to deliver instruction, the greater the variety of engaging learning experiences we can offer to students. The closer we align learning modalities with those preferred by our learners, the more motivated they will be to use them.

Account Settings

In your Zoom account, under In Meeting (Basic), click to "Allow meeting participants to send a message visible to all participants."

It's your option to also select "Prevent participants from saving chat." I recommend this setting unless everyone is aware that all chats can be saved. Whether chats are saved only by the instructor or by all participants, it's very important that **all students be aware that private chats they conduct with individual students or with the instructor will be saved in the Chat transcripts and will be visible to everyone** who can access them.

There are times when you will want all participants to be able to save chat, for example, when it contains valuable information shared or processed during the class meeting that all students should be able to access. If you want students to access the chat thread after the class meeting, you can allow saved chats or copy key information to the CMS. Some active chat structures provide an opportunity for students to review chats and vote on responses, and some chat threads will contain important information for a later review of class topics. Participants can manually save chats before the close of the class meeting, or each participant can select the option for Auto-Saving Chats in their individual account settings.

Under the next setting, Private Chat, select "Allow meeting participants to send a private 1:1 message to another participant." This can be deactivated inside the meeting but cannot be activated in the meeting unless it is already enabled in Settings before the start of the meeting. Remember, inform users that "private chat" sent during class is not private since it is visible to anyone with access to the chat transcript.

The next setting allows you to save the meeting chats for yourself as the host. You activate "Auto saving chats: Automatically save all in-meeting chats so that hosts do not need to manually save the text of the chat after the meeting starts." Once activated, this provides a file after the meeting with a record of the chat content. If you have asked for feedback, or attendees have sent you questions or comments through Chat, it's a good idea to enable this feature to be able to easily access the content without keeping the meeting open. The chats will otherwise disappear after you end the meeting.

To allow attached files to be sent through Chat, select "Both the Hosts and participants can send files through the in-meeting chat." You can specify the file types allowed if you wish.

Meeting Controls

During the class meeting, click *Chat* and when the Chat window appears on the right side of the meeting screen, click on the three dots to the right of *File*. This will allow you to select "Participant can chat with" No One, Host Only, Everyone Publicly, Everyone Publicly and Privately. See the Active Chat Structures in the following section for more details on when to use each Chat setting.

Tech and Meeting Support

If you have a designated instructor or technical support co-host for your classroom, you can ask attendees to direct their questions to the co-host, who can manage problems with access or meeting controls. It's also helpful to provide an email address (or phone number to send a text or call) in case attendees are bumped from the meeting and cannot rejoin. Be sure to check the email inbox or phone for text messages from students who have been bumped from the meeting and cannot rejoin.

If you do not have an instructor or technical support co-host, you might ask students about their level of technology proficiency, then request that one (or more) serve as Zoom "Tech" Ambassadors (thanks to Lené Whitley-Putz at Foothill College for this term), helping other students solve issues that might arise. If the problems prove to be more complex, time-consuming, or beyond the capacity of the Ambassador to solve, the Ambassador can redirect the questions to you through Chat so that you can take immediate action, or address the issue during the next student-led activity or during a formal break.

1. Networking Chats

A Networking Chat can offer an opportunity to address the Social Zoom fatigue that can arise from students feeling disconnected from other learners. Marissa Shuffler, an associate professor at Clemson University, studies workplace wellbeing and teamwork effectiveness. She recommends creating opportunities on Zoom for personal connection: "Spend some time to actually check into people's wellbeing. . .It's a way to reconnect us with the world, and to maintain trust and reduce fatigue and concern" (https://www.bbc.com/worklife/article/20200421-why-zoom-video-chats-are-so-exhausting). The Chat setting, "Participant can chat with Everyone Publicly and Privately" needs to be enabled in the Chat meeting settings.

> **Class Break Chats:** You can use this activity to allow students to chat with each other about any topic they choose, simply to socialize and connect. This can take place before the start of class once you begin allowing students in from the Waiting Room, during the formal breaks if you request that students connect with another student during the upcoming break, or at the end of class if you build in time for the meeting to run after the formal class instruction period ends.
>
> **In-Class Chats:** You can schedule short, five-minute social chat sessions interspersed throughout the class. These social chat sessions can be through private individual chats or through public group chats that are sent and read by the entire class. Using public chats sent to everyone is a great way to ensure that some learners are not left out of the interaction if they don't know anyone in the class, since the comments are addressed to everyone in the class and anyone can respond. You can also use assigned Pair (or Trio) Chats to encourage social chatting (see Page 16). The networking chats can be very informal, casual, and freewheeling.
>
> **Guided Networking Chats** use focus or starter questions, and they can be Topic-Based Focus Questions or Social Networking Starter questions.

Topic-Based Focus Questions

Automotive Mechanics: If you could design your own car, what features would it have?

Hospitality Management: If you were to focus on event management in your career, what kinds of events do you find most interesting?

Social Networking Starter Questions

Are you able to visit with family members in person? Through Zoom?

What artists or kinds of music do you most enjoy? (or) What are the top three songs on your playlist right now, and what do you like about them?

How do you feel about critical events (important to you) going on in this country or in the world right now?

2. Instructor Question Chats

These chats allow the instructor to ask students to direct questions only to the instructor during the main room sessions. Multiple questions can then be asked in a discrete manner at any time. You can answer questions immediately by either speaking or chatting to the entire group if relevant to all, or simply send an individual (or group) reply when you are next able (without distracting yourself while attempting to explain a concept to students or leading an activity). It's important to let students know that you are receiving questions and will be answering them ASAP, otherwise they will be likely to quit sending questions. The Chat setting, "Participant can chat with Host Only" needs to be enabled in the Chat meeting settings.

Of course, students can also ask questions in main room sessions by raising a hand, using the Raise Hand feature. During a meeting, they can click on the icon labeled "Participants" at the bottom center of the meeting controls. At the bottom of the window on the right side of the screen, they then click the button labeled "Raise Hand." Students who have used the Raise Hand feature rise to the top of the Participants listing so the instructor can see and call on them more easily.

Students can also literally raise a hand in a smaller meeting where all participants are visible to the instructor. They can also unmute themselves to ask a question. Remember, all questions are important questions, and learners should be encouraged to ask questions using various methods. The additional use of Chat for questions offers the instructor the ability to manage the stream of questions, to determine which ones to answer and in what order, and to more closely align the question topics with the material being presented and discussed.

3. Instructor Read-Aloud Chats

The Read-Aloud Chats can be used to share student ideas, feedback, questions, and responses sent through Chat. You request a response sent privately to you through Chat, then as responses come in, you can read them aloud to the group, stopping at the end to comment. If you request questions, you can read them aloud, then answer questions as they are posted, or wait to see which questions are most frequent and read and answer those. The Chat setting, "Participant can chat with Host Only" needs to be enabled in the Chat meeting settings.

Graphic Design: Which of these two logos displaying now (using Share Screen) would you select to present to a client? Why is it a better design?

Commercial Electrician: What questions do you have about the proper installation of a Service Disconnect?

4. Assigned Paired Chats

You can use Assigned Paired Chats to create conversations inside the main session room. The Chat setting, "Participant can chat with Everyone Publicly and Privately" needs to be enabled in the Chat meeting settings. In order to pair students, you can use various options.

1. **Pre-Assigned Learning Partners:** The instructor can assign pairings at the start of the term. Simply create a spreadsheet from the class roster and divide it into two equal columns with names across from each other shown as chat Learning Partners. During any class period you can ask these pairs to do an activity with their learning partner. They remain paired throughout the term and often become very comfortable working with each other.
2. **Random Pairings:** Using the same class roster spreadsheet, change the order of names in one of the columns each time to randomly reassign chat partners. Display the random pairings using Share Screen (or on a Google Sheet) and ask students to chat (privately) only with their partner. Remind them that their "private" chats are available for viewing by anyone with access to the Chat transcript.

The assigned paired chats are focused on key topics and concepts from the course.

Criminal Justice: What are the key differences between a mediation and an arbitration? Who is typically present at each proceeding? What are the differences in preparation?

Veterinary Technician: What are the protocols for medication and fluid administration? What problems might arise during these procedures? How might you best respond to these problems?

5. Reporting Chats

These chats allow learners to report out from an inquiry group, either from a prior group assignment out of class, an in-class chat, or from a completed Breakout Room activity. Be sure to ask that students select a spokesperson before beginning their group activity. This person can then take some notes and be able to report out when they return.

Each reporter is asked to post their findings or conclusions in the chat, and these can be either sent to the instructor privately or shared with their entire class. The instructor can comment on findings or request that other students comment through a class discussion. The Chat setting, "Participant can chat with Everyone Publicly and Privately" needs to be enabled in the Chat meeting settings.

6. Feedback Chats

Try using Feedback Chats to encourage peer feedback on assignments in process, class progress, or other topics. The instructor assigns pairs, trios, or teams, then supplies a specific feedback question. The Chat setting, "Participant can chat with Everyone Publicly and Privately" needs to be enabled in the Chat meeting settings.

Geography: Send your partner a copy of the current draft of your Weather Forecasting Model project (use attached file in Chat). Each partner reviews the other partner's model, then uses Chat to comment on the following:

1. What other businesses beyond the ones identified in the report might be impacted by the model they selected?
2. What revisions can be made to strengthen the section assessing the prediction accuracy of the model?
3. What revisions can be made to strengthen the section suggesting changes that may need to be made to the model to account for the impacts of climate change?

Class Progress: Use Chat to ask your partner the following questions, then provide feedback (including questions, suggestions, and observations) on their responses, sending them at least a 50-word response to each of these questions (use a word-count tool in an Office app or Google Doc):

1. In which graded area of the course (homework, quizzes, projects) are you feeling most confident so far, and why?
2. What is the greatest obstacle to your success in this course?
3. What resources might best help you address the obstacle you identified in question 2?
4. What is your level of motivation to utilize these resources (1—very low to 10—very high)?

7. Practice Chats

Practice Chats can be used to give students an opportunity for skill practice. They can do so with explanations and roleplays, among other practice opportunities. The Chat setting, "Participant can chat with Everyone Publicly and Privately" needs to be enabled in the Chat meeting settings.

> **Economics:** Partner 1: Explain in a chat exchange with your partner the concept of "Opportunity Cost." Offer an example from the business world, then a second example from your personal life (like choosing to attend a party versus having dinner with other friends). Partner 2: For each chat sent/posted, respond with a specific, focused question that invites your partner to explain further or to give more examples. Switch roles after 5 minutes, then Partner 2: Explain in a chat exchange with your partner the concept of "Social Contract Theory," with each partner following the directions above.

> **Pharmacy Technician:** Conduct a roleplay in which one student acts as a patient (not using student's actual health records) and the other takes the role of the pharmacy technician. The technician acquires the patient contact information, allergies to medications, and HIPAA compliance approval, then provides medication instructions and answers patient questions.

> **Hospitality Management:** Conduct a roleplay in which one student acts as an unhappy client whose wedding catering did not go well when the food arrived late and is demanding a full refund. The other student, acting as the caterer, attempts to explain the mishap and negotiates a reasonable solution that will satisfy the client.

8. Quiz Chats

To create an opportunity for retrieval practice, sharpen understanding of key concepts and help students consolidate long-term memory, try using Quiz Chats. The instructor first requests students to develop a small set of quiz questions (up to 10) based on prior assigned reading or class content, then the quiz chats can be conducted in numerous ways shown below. The instructor can choose to assign differing topics to avoid overlap in questions. The Chat setting, "Participant can chat with Everyone Publicly and Privately" needs to be enabled in the Chat meeting settings.

> **Assigned Pair Quiz Chat:** The instructor uses Share Screen to show assigned pairs on a spreadsheet or shares them through a Google Sheet.

The assigned pairs alternate sending quiz questions and commenting on the answer from the other student. If the answer is correct, the student sending a quiz question can verify it's correct (and celebrate, using Replies or Reactions to send Emoticons or animated GIFs). If not correct, the student can encourage another attempt. They can then supply the correct answer (and why).

Student-Generated Quiz Chat: The instructor assigns one student at a time to send a quiz chat question to the entire group. This can be conducted as a game in which the first student to answer correctly then sends a new question to the class. The instructor can also increase participation by asking that all students wait a certain time period (determined by the complexity of generating an answer to the question) and then send a response to the instructor. The instructor can select from among the correct answers to ask that this student then send the class the next quiz question. The instructor can respond to other students who answered incorrectly (individually) or look for patterns in incorrect responses and discuss these answers with the entire class, verbally or through chat.

Instructor-Generated Quiz Chat: The instructor sends a quiz chat question to the entire group. As with the student-generated quiz chat, this can also be conducted as a game in which the first student to answer correctly then sends a question to the class. See options in above section.

Student-to-Student Quiz Chats: Students are paired and asked to develop quiz questions, then they take turns quizzing each other through chat.

> **Spanish:** Both students prepare a list of 10 vocabulary words and definitions, with examples, before class. They can be from different assignments/chapters to ensure no overlap in quiz questions. In pairs, students alternate sending a word and requesting their partner to define the word and give an example (in a more advanced class, the explanation can be in Spanish). If their partner is unable to define or supply an example, the first student sends the definition and example they prepared earlier.

> **Biology:** Both students prepare a list of 10 quiz questions on bacteria types and cell structure. In pairs, students alternate sending a question and requesting their partner to provide a specific answer and an example or explanation. If their partner is unable to answer correctly, or supply the example or explanation, the first student sends the answer, example, or explanation, or instead they could work through the problem together before moving to the next quiz question.

9. Debate Chats

Debate Chats are used to engage students more fully in a topic by taking sides in a debate format. The Chat setting, "Participant can chat with Everyone Publicly and Privately" needs to be enabled in the Chat meeting settings.

Assigned Pair Debate Chat: The instructor uses Share Screen to show assigned pairs on a spreadsheet or shares them through a Google Sheet. The two students hold their own mini-debate for a timed period, following a set of rules for time use and argument protocol supplied by the instructor. After the end of the debate, another option is for the students to submit their chat debate to a third party, instructor or student, to declare a winner. A rubric supplied by the instructor is helpful in assessing the debate results. The instructor (or student) can also do this later by reviewing the Chat transcript if the instructor has activated the meeting setting: "Auto saving chats: Automatically save all in-meeting chats so that hosts do not need to manually save the text of the chat after the meeting starts."

Whole Class Debate Chat: The instructor uses Share Screen to show assigned teams and differing debate topics on a spreadsheet (or shares them through a Google Sheet), with half of the class on one team and the second half on the other team. The class instructor chooses who goes first from Team 1, followed by another student from Team 2. Each student provides a debate argument or counterargument, and class teams debate for a timed period, following a set of rules for time use and argument protocol supplied by the instructor. After the end of the debate, the instructor can declare a winner or offer feedback on each team's arguments.

Observed Team Debates: Assigned pairs or larger teams prepare their arguments in advance (or shorter debate format if given time only during class to prepare) on differing debate topics. The instructor chooses which pairing or teams go first. Each paired student or opposing team provides a debate argument or counterargument and debates for a timed period, following a set of rules for time use and argument protocol supplied by the instructor. After the end of each timed debate, the observing students use a Poll or vote through Chat to declare a winner, or can offer feedback on each team's arguments.

Journalism: Which of the following is the most valuable form of news media?

1) Print newspapers, 2) Magazines, 3) News agencies, 4) Broadcast journalism, 5) Online journalism, 6) Photojournalism, 7) Alternative media, or 8) Online newspapers.

U.S. Government: Argue whether Washington D.C. should (or should not) become the 51st state. Address issues such as voting representation, population size compared to other states, the 23rd Amendment, Article 1: Section 8 of the Constitution, and retrocession, among others.

10. Whole Group Chats

Try Whole Group Chats to encourage students to share their ideas with the entire group. Unlike the in-person classroom, where everyone calling out answers simultaneously might make it difficult to hear any one student's ideas, this format allows learners to view a wide variety of contributions with differing perspectives. The Chat setting, "Participant can chat with Everyone Publicly and Privately" needs to be enabled first.

There's great value in learners' exposure to numerous ideas, both in seeing their perspectives reinforced as well as considering perspectives they would not have generated themselves. Although the chat stream fills quickly, and numerous chats can be hard to absorb, the viewer can manage their intake of ideas by scrolling through at their own pace.

I recommend giving at least two to three minutes to participants to view the chats (depending on meeting size) and to encourage a deeper interaction with the ideas than might happen through causal chat on their phone. They might be asked to select one idea that interests them, then send one response to the entire group. To further the conversation, they could also be asked to select an idea that most interests them, then begin a chat only with the person who posted the idea, allowing five minutes for individual conversations to take place.

11. Forwarding Chats

To use Forwarding Chats, ask students to send their ideas, responses to questions, or other contributions to the instructor only, then select a limited number to copy/paste and forward, sending to all participants. Unlike Whole Group Chats, the instructor serves as a filter, forwarding only a handful of responses, and the learners can then focus only on this limited sample of responses. The instructor can look for examples of similar patterns of responses, diversity in perspectives, or comments that allow the instructor to make connections to the lesson content or draw out critical main points. The Chat setting, "Participant can chat with Host only" needs to be enabled first.

Chat forwarding can also be used when a student contributes an idea during a class lesson, but the student doesn't want to unmute and speak this idea out loud. The instructor can request that students indicate whether their chat shares to the instructor are anonymous (or not), and the instructor has the option to credit the specific student when forwarding the idea to the group. The Chat setting, "Participant can chat with Everyone Publicly and Privately" needs to be enabled in the Chat meeting settings.

PREVENTING ISSUES AND TROUBLESHOOTING

1. If you use varied active Chat structures during a single class period, be certain to check (and change) the in-meeting Chat settings if needed to align with the upcoming structure. Select Chat, then click on the three dots . . .
2. When you complete a chat with an "Everyone Publicly, or Everyone Publicly and Privately" activity, be certain to reset to "Participant can chat with Host Only" if you don't want student side-chatting during the next activity.
3. Request that everyone stay audio muted during a chat activity unless it is a mixed activity with combined chat and discussion.

REFERENCE

1. "How many texts do people send every day?" (2018). Posted on May 18, 2016 by Kenneth Burke Blog Post, https://www.textrequest.com/blog.

Breakout Rooms

BREAKOUT ROOMS

Though Zoom offers us an alternative classroom space, the main feature of Zoom—the collective meeting room with sometimes faceless participants—doesn't replicate the small-group work that many instructors use to engage learners. In fact, since Zoom elevates the meeting host and privileges the speaker, in some ways the technology replicates a teacher-centric class structure.

In our face-to-face classes, many of us recognize it is essential for students to participate in active learning for them to be able to reach measurable learning outcomes. Numerous recent studies have concluded that active learning is far more effective than a traditional lecture. A 2014 meta-analysis of 225 studies on test scores and failure rates of STEM (science, technology, engineering, mathematics) students showed that students in lecture classes were 1.5 times more likely to fail than were students in active learning classes.

23

Students in active learning classes demonstrated higher average examination scores (Freeman et al., 2014).

One way to encourage active learning is to have students *doing*—speaking, writing, analyzing, and creating—rather than passively listening. In large classes, only one person (teacher or student) can speak at a time, but we can easily ask students to turn their chairs and work together in smaller groups. So, what's the Zoom equivalent of dragging chairs into a smaller huddle? Zoom Breakout Rooms offer an excellent opportunity for active learning. These rooms are the most engaging feature of Zoom and can be used in multiple ways. Breakout Rooms are an effective tool in ensuring active learning is taking place during a class meeting.

As physics Nobel Prize winner Carl Wieman has said, "At the college level, the evidence is clear: science students learn less when they are expected to listen passively." Although material can be introduced, summarized, or further explored in brief lectures, these lectures should be punctuated by frequent opportunities for students to engage with the material. This is especially true for distance learning when the potential for numerous distractions is heightened. The Breakout Rooms are ideal for active engagement. As Wieman describes active learning, "Rather than listening passively, students spend class time engaged in answering questions, solving problems, discussing solutions with their peers and reasoning about the material they are studying, all while getting regular feedback from their teacher. . .complex learning, including scientific thinking, requires the extended practice and interaction. . .to literally rewire the brain to take on new capabilities" (2014).

The active synchronous Zoom learning structures and discipline-specific examples in this chapter promote active learning. They offer students an opportunity to answer questions, solve problems, discuss solutions with their peers, and reason about the material they are studying, all while getting regular feedback from their instructor.

The instructor can create up to 50 Breakout Rooms with a maximum per Breakout Room (up to 200) determined by the type of plan. Breakout Room participants can use Share Screen to share video, audio, and Whiteboard annotations.

In order to help students get more value in the Breakout Rooms, it's helpful for the instructor to review the activity directions before opening the rooms. Ask to see if there are any questions about the directions before they leave the Main Session Room. Remind students that if they need help, they can request that the instructor visit their Breakout Room using the Ask for Help option. They can also leave the Breakout Room to return to the Main Session Room, speak with the instructor, and then can be added back to the

Breakout Room by the Host. Broadcast a "One Minute Remaining" message as a heads-up to complete the activity.

To support students in completing the activity:

- Send directions through Chat **before opening** the Breakout Rooms (since Chat won't reach into the Breakout Rooms from the Main Session Room). You can also email them.
- Broadcast a message to the Breakout Rooms while they are in session. If it is a multipart activity, timed with specific break points when students need to change roles or switch activities, you can set a timer to remind you to broadcast a message reminding them to switch roles/activities. You can also broadcast a "2 Minutes Remaining" message as a heads-up to wrap up the activity.
- Post directions on their course site inside the current module or send as an announcement.

Account Settings

Under In Meeting (Basic), select "Allow host to split meeting participants into separate, smaller rooms." Also select "Allow host to assign participants to breakout rooms when scheduling." If you have regular meetings of paired Learning Partners, Project Teams, or Jigsaw Home Groups, you can set these pre-assigned groups up when scheduling the meeting, then easily drop students into these groups in a Breakout Room at any time during the class meeting. It's much faster than manually assigning students into rooms, and you can use both the pre-assigned groups as well as new randomly selected groups within the same meeting.

It can sometimes be challenging to set up the pre-assigned teams since students need to have a Zoom account. Not all Zoom accounts appear to work with the pre-assigned teams. If students log into the Zoom meeting with a different email address than the one they originally used to create their personal account, they won't appear in the pre-assigned team during the meeting. If students have a college-assigned Zoom account, or their access to Zoom is integrated with the course management system, it may not be recognized as their having a personal Zoom account, and they can't be placed in the pre-assigned team.

Warning: If you select "Remote support: Allow meeting host to provide 1:1 remote support to another participant," *the Breakout Rooms and Simultaneous Screen Sharing will be deactivated*. Remote Support is helpful to assist a remote user to share their desktop so you can problem solve together.

Meeting Controls

Only the host can assign participants to Breakout Rooms. The co-host can leave and join any Breakout Room only if they initially join a Breakout Room assigned to them by the host. To assign students to Breakout Rooms, select the Breakout Room bottom tab. Choose whether to have Zoom randomly assign "Automatically" or whether you want to "Manually" assign students to rooms. If you have pre-assigned groups, you will also see that option. Select the number of rooms that allows for the total number of participants you want to assign to each room. Select "Create Breakout Rooms," then adjust assignments to rooms as needed. You can also rename rooms (from Breakout Room 1) to a topic or team room name (like Team Blue or Exploring Planets).

Under "Options," you can "Allow participants to return to the main session at any time" so that they can return and ask questions of the instructor. You can select a pre-assigned room closure time for rooms to close automatically (with an extra time's-up notification sent to the host), or keep time yourself and manually close the rooms. You can also set the countdown timer that will allow learners to wrap up their activity when the rooms are closing.

Once the rooms are assigned, you can first give students directions for their activity, answer questions, then "Open All Rooms" to begin the activity. Watch to see if any student has not joined their Breakout Room, and check with them to see if they need help. After an activity has ended, you can send student groups back into the same rooms, or select "Recreate" to assign students to new rooms with a different group.

---

1. Icebreakers

Icebreakers can be used at the start of any new class term, class period, or before the class moves to a new topic. They allow students to make a rapid connection with a small subset of the class and warm them up to collaborating, connecting with others and to the upcoming topic. Directions for the activities can be announced by the instructor, shared though Chat, displayed through Share Screen, entered in a Google Doc, or Broadcast into the Breakout Rooms.

Two Truths and a Lie is frequently offered as an icebreaker. First create random Breakout Room groups of three to four students (larger groups increase activity time and decrease engagement). Provide the following directions to start the activity: "Everyone will have 2 minutes to write down in your notes three statements about yourself. Two statements are true and the other is a lie. To make this a little more fun, try adding in a true statement that nobody might guess about you, as long as you are comfortable sharing it." Provide a demo by offering three statements about yourself, two truths and a lie. Ask students to guess which is the lie. You can create a Poll in advance for this, or use Chat for student responses. Then allow the two minutes for students to create their own.

Provide the following directions before opening the Breakout Rooms: "Each participant, one at a time, share the three statements with the group in your Breakout Room. Two statements are true and the other is a lie. The other students in the group attempt to guess which statement is the lie. You will have two minutes per person, for a total of eight minutes (if groups of four)." Broadcast a message when there are two minutes remaining, then close the Breakout Rooms.

Stranded on an Island offers an opportunity for students to identify what's important to them. Ask students the question, "What are three things that you would take with you if you were stranded on a remote island and couldn't leave for years, or ever?" Provide a demo by sharing your answer with the students. Tell them: "You have two minutes to write down in your notes the three things that you would take with you if you were going to be stranded on a remote island."

Provide the following directions before opening the Breakout Rooms: "Each participant, one at a time, share the three things you would take to the island with the group in your Breakout Room. Each student also asks one question of another student about one of their three items. You will have two minutes per person, including sharing the three items and answering the question, for a total of eight minutes (if groups of four)." Broadcast a message when there are two minutes remaining, then close the Breakout Rooms.

Shared and Unique allows students to discover what they have in common, as well as what characteristics are unique to each student. Give students the directions, "When you get to your Breakout Rooms, work with your partners to identify three things that everyone in the group shares, and everyone write them down. Avoid the obvious like, 'We all breathe oxygen,' or 'We are all taking this class.' Then identify one thing that is unique about each student." Provide a demo by sharing a possible outcome, for example, "Maybe every student was born outside of the state they live in now, has a pet in their home, and has worked in the food industry in the past. And perhaps, for example, Student 1 is the only one who has three brothers, Student 2 plays on the women's soccer team, Student 3 comes from a bilingual household, and Student 4 is a parent with a young child."

Provide the following directions before opening the Breakout Rooms: "Everyone work together to identify and write down the three things shared in common and the one thing that is unique about each student. Avoid the obvious and use different characteristics from the demo I shared. You will have a total of 10 minutes." Broadcast a message when there are 2 minutes remaining, then close the Breakout Rooms.

Find the Error is an icebreaker activity that focuses on warming learners up to a concept within the course discipline. The instructor creates a one-page document that is shared with the group (attached Chat file or Google Doc). The document contains information about a key class topic, but the instructor has introduced "errors" or incorrect information in the summary of findings.

Archaeology: For example, the instructor might create a summary of the findings from the Olduvai Gorge in Tanzania, where *Homo Habilis* was discovered, the 2 million–year-old ancestor of *Homo Sapiens*. If the topic is being introduced for the first time, the "errors" to be discovered in the summary of findings can be much more basic and more obvious to students without much background knowledge. Otherwise, students with a more advanced understanding can be challenged to work together to find more complex errors in the summary.

Provide the following directions before opening the Breakout Rooms: "Review (solo) the summary of findings for 5 minutes, then I will place you in Breakout Rooms to work together to create a list of the 'errors' in the summary. There are five errors to discover. You will have a total of 10 minutes working in the Breakout Room. All participants should be prepared to report out when you return." Broadcast a message when there are two minutes remaining, then close the Breakout Rooms.

2. Collaborative Quizzes

Quizzes create another opportunity for retrieval practice, sharpening understanding of key concepts, and consolidating long-term memory. The opportunity for collaboration also lowers the stakes on testing, reducing test anxiety, and creating improved conditions for learning. Using collaborative quizzes as preparation for later testing has been shown to lead to more positive student attitudes about both the subject matter and their peers. Students who engaged in collaborative testing also reported completing more assigned readings and developed more positive attitudes toward their learning, the testing process, and the class subject (Slusser, Erickson, 2006). Collaborative quizzes can be counted toward an individual student grade or used as practice quizzes that will then prepare students for future individual testing.

The instructor should develop quizzes using any preferred method (test banks of written questions to be shared through Google Docs or an attached Chat file, or tests created in apps such as Socrative or Kahoot!). In my experience, using testing apps is preferred by students and offers the instructors more options for delivering and processing testing. The quiz should be short enough to be completed in no more than 10 to 20 minutes. If you have more material than this, consider breaking a longer quiz into two shorter quizzes to allow learners to sustain focus.

Written Quiz Questions: Provide the following directions before opening the Breakout Rooms: "Open the attached file in Chat containing your quiz for today. In groups of three, everyone work together to answer the quiz questions. Be sure to discuss the questions and possible answers before selecting your final answer. All students should write down their answers and then submit them (Chat, email, or assignment submission box) after returning to the main session room. You will have a total of 15 minutes." Broadcast a message when there are 2 minutes remaining, then close the Breakout Rooms.

The instructor can review the quiz questions and answers immediately afterwards, or grade and return quizzes later, or conduct a class review during the next class meeting.

App-Based Quizzes: Provide the following directions before opening the Breakout Rooms: "I am sending you the link through Chat for a [Socrative, Kahoot!, other app] quiz. When you arrive at the Breakout Room, log in to the quiz, and once everyone is in, begin the quiz. In groups of three or four, everyone work together to answer the quiz questions. Be sure to discuss the questions and possible answers before selecting your final answer. You will have a total of 15 minutes." Students can all supply answers to just a single open group quiz, or they can work together to determine answers, with each student entering the final answer on their individual quiz. Broadcast a message when there are 2 minutes remaining, then close the Breakout Rooms.

The advantage of a quiz app is that the instructor can review the quiz questions and answers immediately afterwards, using Share Screen to show the questions and results. Then the instructor can address the questions with the fewest correct answers, reviewing the correct answers and explaining why or showing how to solve the problems. The instructor can also ask students who correctly answered to share their approach or reasoning.

App-Based Competitive Team Quizzes: Students can also collaborate within testing teams to compete against other teams. This also leverages the practice of gamification, the introduction of game elements into nongame situations. Some research has shown that gamification in learning experiences increases engagement, motivation, and performance (Faiella and Ricciardi, 2015). Kahoot! is ideal for a learning game format, and Socrative includes the option of running "Space Race," pitting teams against each other during the quiz. See Chapter 8 for more details on apps.

With Socrative's "Space Race" format, you can start a countdown just before the start of the activity, using Share Screen to show the rockets representing each team's performance ready to blast off. Then provide the following directions before opening the Breakout Rooms: "I am sending you the link through Chat for a [Socrative, Kahoot, other app] quiz. When you arrive at the Breakout Room, **only one student will log in to the quiz,** and then this student should use Share Screen to show everyone the quiz questions. In teams of three, everyone work together to answer the quiz questions. Be sure to discuss the questions and possible answers before selecting your final answer. You will have a total of [10–15] minutes." Broadcast a reminder message when there are 2 minutes remaining (though the quiz should show them time remaining), then close the Breakout Rooms.

You can review the quiz questions and answers immediately afterwards, using Share Screen to show the questions and results. Then you can address the questions with the fewest correct answers, reviewing the correct answers and explaining why or showing how to solve the problems. You can also ask students who correctly answered to share their approach or reasoning.

3. Learning Partner Activities

Having a learning partner assigned for an entire term offers an opportunity for increased collaboration, accountability, and support. Learning partners can come together for brief meetings or longer processing. They can be asked to support each other in numerous ways, including these:

- Getting started on new assignments
- Checking progress on assignments in process
- Consolidating new learning
- Testing each other's knowledge and understanding of key concepts
- Reviewing assignments and projects to provide feedback for revision
- Reflecting on completed assignments or learning modules
- Using metacognitive strategies to reflect on learning approaches

Nutritional Science: Following a lesson on protein digestion, absorption, and metabolism, ask Learning Partners to work together in Breakout Rooms. They should help each other understand the recent lesson by explaining to each other how proteins from foods get processed into amino acids that cells can use to make new proteins. The learning partners record any questions they still have about the process and return to the main room to ask the instructor their questions.

Legal Studies: Before a new module on U.S. Immigration Policy and Citizenship, the Learning Partners work together in Breakout Rooms to preview one of the major provisions of the Immigration and Nationality Act. Each Learning Partner pair is assigned a different topic to preview, including:

- Family-based immigration
- Employment-based immigration
- Per-country ceilings
- Refugees and asylees
- The Diversity Visa Program
- Temporary Protected Status (TPS)
- Deferred Action for Childhood Arrivals (DACA)

Marine Biology: Ask Learning Partners to work together in Breakout Rooms for a Guided Reflection on their recently completed Coral Reef Ecosystems projects. The Guided Reflection questions could include the following:

1. What discoveries did you make about recent changes in coral reef population biology?
2. Which of the following did you conclude posed the greatest danger to coral reef ecosystems?

   a. coral mining
   b. pollution (organic and nonorganic)
   c. overfishing
   d. blast fishing
   e. warming oceans

3. What was the most difficult part of your project, and why?
4. What changes could you make to your approach to do even better on the upcoming Marine Mammal Biology project?

4. Observer Trios

These trio groupings are useful because they include an observer who can provide feedback on the active pairing in the Breakout Room. Before going into the rooms, each student is assigned a role. Two of the students engage in a paired learning activity while the third student observes and takes notes to share with the pairing when they complete their work. If time allows, the students can switch roles so that all three in the trio take a turn as the observer. The observer can provide feedback on the accuracy of the pair's understanding or explanation of ideas, feedback on the effectiveness of the pair's interaction, or scoring or rating of the pair's practicing specific skills.

> **Marketing:** After a module on Brand Management, provide students with a handout about how to measure the outcomes of brand management strategies. The components might include the following:
>
> 1. **Brand Awareness:** Familiarity of both general public and target audience with brand
> 2. **Brand Equity:** Consumer perception of the value of the brand, impacting pricing
> 3. **Brand Loyalty:** Willingness of customers to commit to brand and buy repeatedly
> 4. **Brand Recognition:** How well consumers recognize your brand's attributes like logo, advertising, and so on
> 5. **Brand Reputation:** Whether the general public/target audience has a favorable view of your brand

Provide all students with a case study describing a company with brand management problems. Assign one student to be a representative of the company, another to be a marketing consultant, and the third to be the observer. Once in the Breakout Room, the marketing consultant should explain to the company representative how to better manage their brand, recommending some specific strategies to address one or more of the five areas. The observer should watch, listen, and take notes on a rubric using categories that measure the effectiveness of the marketing consultant's interaction with the company representative.

Using the same company case study, or a new case study, the trio can then change roles. During the three rounds, each student has a chance to play each role. Upon return to the main session room, the class can discuss brand management challenges and solutions.

Ethnic Studies/Sociology: After a module on Racial Profiling, provide students with two handouts to review. Handout 1 contains statistics regarding racial factors playing a role in traffic stops, denial of retail services, immigration enforcement actions, street policing policies, housing access, mortgage discrimination, and so on. Handout 2 contains real-life stories regarding the experiences of people who have been racially profiled in traffic stops, denial of retail services, immigration enforcement actions, street policing policies, housing access, mortgage discrimination, and so forth. Assign Student 1 in each Breakout Room to review Handout 1 and Student 2 to review Handout 2. Student 3 will be the observer. Once in the room, Student 1 uses the data to persuade the Observer of the existence of racial profiling. Then Student 2 uses the stories to persuade the Observer of the existence of racial profiling. When students return from the Breakout Rooms, ask the Observers to share their experience as to whether they were more persuaded of the existence of racial profiling by the data or by the stories.

Religious Studies: After a module on Reincarnation in World Religions, provide students with a comparative handout for initial review. After the review period is ended, assign two students in each Breakout Room to alternate describing the concept of Reincarnation in 8 to 10 world religions, both major and smaller. The third student should be the observer and scorekeeper. The observer should have a more detailed comparative handout that can be used to assess the accuracy of the student descriptions, and the observer should determine a score between 1 and 10 for each student description, using the criteria of accuracy and completeness. When students return from the Breakout Rooms, ask the Observers to nominate a top-scoring description and have that student share their description with the entire class.

5. Read-Arounds

Any content that requires a high level of student attention can benefit from a shared reading. You can use PowerPoint or a shared document to provide directions before sending students to Breakout Rooms to do their reading. The readings, spoken out loud, should be no longer than 5 to 10 minutes to ensure sustained focus. Identify the reading material and how it will be divided between the readers, ensuring that each reader has an opportunity to read a roughly equivalent amount. A shorter reading can be divided into three or four sections, one section for each student in the Breakout Room. A longer reading can simply continue around the room, with each reader reading only one paragraph or section until the group reaches the end of the reading.

English as a Second Language: Assign three students to each Breakout Room. Before opening the rooms, send a one-page handout (three paragraphs) with an assigned reading as an attached Chat file. Ask students to open the file and be sure they all can access it. Provide them with directions for the activity and allow time to answer their questions about the directions before opening the rooms. Allow at least 20 to 30 minutes for this activity, and visit each room in turn, staying to observe, answer questions, and support them in staying on track.

Once they arrive at the Breakout Room, they should do the following:

1. Each person reads one paragraph out loud to the group. Help each other out with words that are more difficult to pronounce. Read to the end of the page, switching readers for every paragraph.
2. For a second time, each person reads one paragraph out loud to the group. Stop at the end of each paragraph, and in your own words paraphrase the ideas in the paragraph. The group can provide assistance as needed.
3. As a group, find and write down the main point of each paragraph. Continue to the end of the page, with everyone discussing and writing down the main points for all paragraphs. Use other reading strategies you have been taught, like activating prior knowledge, and so on.

Structural Engineering: Assign four students to each Breakout Room. Before opening the rooms, send an attached file through Chat with a short case study handout summarizing a bridge collapse incident (for example, the FIU-Sweetwater University City pedestrian bridge collapsing onto U.S. Route 41 that resulted in six deaths, eight injuries, and eight crushed vehicles). The case study should not include the final determined cause of the incident. Ask students to please not look up the incident on the Internet (which won't be as much fun for them). If this is still a concern, the instructor can supply an invented case study or remove the specific location/name or other identifying details of the actual case study.

In the Breakout Rooms, ask students to take turns reading short sections of the Case Study out loud to the group (five minutes). Individually, they then write down what they believe to be the underlying cause: 1) an engineering flaw in the bridge design, 2) faulty construction, or 3) substandard materials (three minutes).

After the Read-Around, each student has 3 minutes in a Talk-Around to make an argument as to the predicted cause of the collapse. After 20 minutes, the instructor can close the Breakout Rooms, share the report with the actual determined cause of the incident, and discuss the report with the entire class.

Education: Assign four students to each Breakout Room. Before opening the rooms, send an attached file through Chat with an instructor-created handout on the Growth of Virtual Learning, including several processing questions at the bottom (see suggestions below). Before students go to the Breakout Rooms, supply the following directions:

1. Take turns reading paragraphs of the handout out loud to the group until you reach the end of the article. (5 minutes)
2. Select a spokesperson for the group. (1 minute)
3. Answer the questions at the bottom of the handout as a group, with everyone taking notes on your answers. Help prepare the spokesperson to present your group's answers to the entire class upon return. (10 minutes)

When students return from the rooms, each spokesperson will be asked to share the answers from their group. This will result in a whole-class Read-Around, with 10 readers (if 40 students in the class meeting) each reading their responses for one minute. A class discussion is optional after the Read-Around.

Virtual Learning Handout Questions:

1. What skills are required of students for effective Virtual Learning?
2. What are some of the most challenging growth problems faced by virtual learning platforms and educational institutions?
3. What impact will the rapid growth of Virtual Learning have on equitable outcomes in education? Can you identify both positive and negative potential (or actual) outcomes?

6. Talk-Arounds

When students would benefit from a sequential conversation on a focused topic, they can take turns responding to questions, making brief presentations, processing prior learning, sharing a reflection, or offering their opinion on an assigned topic/issue.

Anatomy and Physiology: Assign six students to each Breakout Room. Before opening the rooms, ask each student to first take 10 minutes to review a skeletal system handout on bones of the skull. Once they are in the breakout room, they should use the Whiteboard feature to mark the location of their assigned bones, identify them, and describe their function.

Assigned Skull Bones:

1. Anterior Skull Bones
2. Lateral Skull Bones
3. Posterior Skull Bones
4. Inferior Skull Bones
5. Cranial Skull Bones
6. Orbital Skull Bones

Philosophy: Following a short lecture on Ethics, and leading up to a research paper on the application of Ethics to Actions of Civil Disobedience, assign three students to each Breakout Room. During their Talk-Around, each student should limit their response to 5 minutes. One student should be assigned to serve as a timekeeper, setting a timer for 5 minutes and keeping the group on track to finish in 15 minutes. Ask students to share their answers to the following questions:

1. Is it ethical to break local, state, or federal laws when engaging in civil disobedience?
2. If you believe breaking laws when engaging in civil disobedience to be ethical, under what specific circumstances is it ethical? Provide examples.
3. To what extent do you believe that there are ethical limitations on law-breaking actions when engaging in civil disobedience? Provide examples.

Fire Science: Assign four students in a team to each Breakout Room. Before opening the rooms, share a list of assigned teams, with each team member also being assigned only one of the four Possible Responses from the options below. Ask each student to first take 10 minutes to prepare a 3-minute presentation for a public education forum for local employees about responding to hazardous material spills. Each student will address a different possible response from the list to discuss, and they will explain why the employee should/should not attempt this response. After preparation, they begin their Talk-Around in the room, limiting each explanation to 3 minutes. If there is time at the end, they attempt to reach consensus on the "correct" response.

Possible Responses:

    a. Send someone for help and warn others of the danger.
    b. Move leaking material out of the way.
    c. Move any vehicles far away from the scene.
    d. Try to extinguish the fire to avoid an explosion.

7. Jigsaw Teams

The jigsaw is one of the most widely used collaborative learning structures. It is ideal for topics that can be divided into three or four parts or chunks. Each part/chunk should take no longer than 10 minutes to learn so both the studying and teaching can be done by students during the class meeting. The jigsaw requires advance preparation by the instructor and is one of the more complex active learning structures, especially delivered on Zoom. The time allowed for each step can be adjusted by the instructor. More complex concepts require more time to be reviewed in Expert Groups and taught in the Home Groups.

1. Create a spreadsheet from the class roster and divide it into two equal columns to allow the sheet to be fully visible without scrolling. Break the list into groups of four, and number the partners in each group from 1 to 4 (or vary these directions for groups of three).
2. Prepare material relevant to your course in one-page text and graphic/chart handouts, or use content from short videos (five minutes maximum), accompanied by a summary that reinforces the concepts addressed in the video. Assign the handouts/video clips a number from 1 to 4. Place materials in course management system, email, or send as attached files through Chat.

Use Share Screen to share the spreadsheet and give students the following directions: "We're going to do an activity that will put each of you into a Home Team with three other people. On the list displayed, find your Home Team and write down the name of all the other members of your team. Notice that after your name there is a number. Write down your number. You will need to know your number for this activity. We are going to do a jigsaw activity, and there are four parts. I will preview all four parts."

Part One (Solo in Home Teams): This part takes place in the main session room. You are about to become an expert on one area of the handout

them from 1 (least successful) to 6 (most successful) based on their successful attention to light, composition, and emotion.

Agricultural Studies: After a module on Chemical Use in Farming, provide a handout on the use of Fungicides, Herbicides, Insecticides, Growth Hormones, and Antibiotics. On the next page of the handout, provide information on Organic versus Conventional Farming Practices for crops and animals.

Ask students to rank their position on Conventional versus Organic Farming on a scale of 1 (Conventional is clearly superior) to 10 (Organic is clearly superior), with numbers in between representing a position closer to one or the other practices, though not fully persuaded, or believing that a combination of practices is best. Ask them to consider issues such as Production Cost, Land Productivity, Tillage, Fertilization, Marketing and Distribution, Environmental Impact, Nutritional Value, Product Demand and Pricing, and so on.

Problem-Solving Fishbowls: Create enough assigned Breakout Rooms to place six students in each room (enough for three pairings). If one room has fewer than six, you can ask students to join the fishbowl more than once during the assigned time. Provide a handout with the problems to be solved by the pairs in the fishbowls and allow time for a preview. Then review the directions before opening the rooms.

Mathematics: Set up Breakout Rooms with six students each. Ask two students in each room to be the first pairing in the fishbowl. Show and explain fishbowl directions. Allow 15 minutes for three pairings. Use Chat to send students three practice problems (and a bonus harder-to-solve problem) in Factoring Polynomials. The two students in the fishbowl should work together for 5 minutes to solve the first problem. The other students should only watch and listen and should not speak or share the solution or approach. After 5 minutes, it's time for a new pairing in the fishbowl.

If the first pairing has solved their assigned problem, the second pairing then works together on the second problem. If the first pair did not complete their problem, the second pair attempts to solve the first problem. If time remains, they can move on to the second problem. After 5 minutes, the third pair either finishes the second problem or starts on the third problem. If the fishbowl pairings finish all their problems before the 15 minutes end, they can all work together to attempt to solve the bonus problem.

Theatre and Drama Studies: Set up Breakout Rooms with six students each. Ask two students in each room to be the first pairing in the fishbowl. Show and explain fishbowl directions. Allow 30 minutes for three pairings. Use Chat, email, or a course management system posting to send students a list of three short one-act plays and accompanying scripts. Include a fourth bonus play for a deeper dive for groups that finish early.

Include various genres and forms of theatrical productions: Musicals, Fringe Theatre, Immersive Theatre, Melodrama, Autobiographicals, Comedy, Tragedy, Historical Plays, Solo Theatre, etc. Assign students numbers: there should be two 1s, two 2s, and two 3s in each Breakout Room, and allow students 10 minutes for an initial review. Students assigned #1 should only review Play 1, students assigned #2 should only review Play 2, and students assigned #3 should only review Play 3.

Once in the Breakout Room, the two students starting in the fishbowl should discuss Play 1, and how it might be adapted for a video-platform delivery. They should identify production challenges in adapting the original on-stage format to an online performance, as well as how they would solve those challenges. The challenges could include the following:

- Backgrounds, Greenscreen, and Scenery
- Audio and Video Quality
- Costume Changes and Intermissions
- Doubling or Multiroles
- Audience Interaction
- Technology Constraints

After 10 minutes, two new students enter the Fishbowl and discuss Play 2. After another 10 minutes the last two students enter the Fishbowl and discuss Play 3.

The other students should only watch and listen and should not speak or share solutions. If the fishbowl pairings finish discussing their production challenges before the 30 minutes ends, they can all work together to discuss the bonus more complex Play 4 production (or generate the outline for a new one-act play).

Computer Science: Set up Breakout Rooms with six students each. Ask two students in each room to be the first pairing in the fishbowl. Show and explain fishbowl directions. Allow 30 minutes for three pairings. Use Chat to send students a handout of six Recent Computer Viruses with an explanation of how they function, how to protect against them, or how to respond if a computer is infected. Include a seventh bonus virus for a deeper dive for groups that finish early. Allow students 10 minutes for an initial review. For example, in 2020, some of these viruses were:

- Cyborg Ransomware
- CryptoMix Clop Ransomware
- GoBrut
- Jokeroo
- Trojan Glupteba
- Thanatos Ransomware
- *Bonus Virus ILOVEYOU

Once in the Breakout Room, the two students in the fishbowl should role-play a client and consultant discussing methods to prevent viral attacks. Student 1 in the fishbowl is the client and asks Student 2 how to protect against Virus 1. Student 2, as consultant, explains how Virus 1 operates and how to protect against harm (5 minutes). Then they switch roles. Student 2 in the fishbowl is the client and asks Student 1 how to protect against Virus 2. Student 1, as consultant, explains how Virus 2 operates and how to protect against harm (5 minutes). After 10 minutes, two new students enter the fishbowl and discuss Viruses 3 and 4, switching roles after 5 minutes. After 10 minutes the last two students enter the fishbowl and discuss Viruses 5 and 6, switching roles after 5 minutes.

Reflection Fishbowls: Create enough assigned Breakout Rooms to place six students in each room (enough for three pairings). If one room has fewer than six, you can ask students to join the fishbowl more than once during the assigned time. Provide a prompt with the reflection questions to be answered by the pairs in the fishbowls. Each pairing can answer the same reflection questions, or there can be a new set of reflection questions for each new pairing. Allow time for a preview if desired. Then review the directions before opening the rooms. Shorter reflections can be timed at 5 minutes each (15 minutes total), and longer, deeper reflections at 10 minutes each (30 minutes total).

Architecture: After the completion of a module on Architectural Design Theory, ask this of students in the fishbowl: "Reflecting on the history of modernist design thinking, and the subsequent challenges to modernist design thinking, what impact did community-based design, as well as social movements and countercultures, have on changing design theory?" Each pairing (5 or 10 minutes) can answer the same reflection question, or focus on a new aspect of Architectural Design with a new set of reflection questions. Allow time for a preview if desired before opening the Breakout Rooms. A whole-class discussion following the fishbowls is also an option.

Women's Studies: After the completion of a module on Global Feminism, ask this of students in the fishbowl: "What role do issues such as access to health care, access to education, participation in the local economy, and changing environmental practices have on women's ability to acquire and sustain political power? How do these issues differ across the global communities you have studied, and what do these communities share in common?"

Each pairing (5 or 10 minutes) will answer the same reflection question and can reference issues raised in the prior paired conversations. Allow time for a preview if desired, before opening the Breakout Rooms. A whole-class discussion following the fishbowls is also an option.

Dance: After the completion of a module on Dance Choreography, send students a Chat with three questions:

1. What are key differences of improvisation and planned choreography for choreographers, directors, and dancers?
2. How do these two approaches impact resulting dance phrases?
3. What are some of your experiences with improvisation and planned choreography as a dance or audience member at performances?

Assign each fishbowl pairing a number, with two 1s, two 2s and two 3s. The pairs with the same number will meet in the fishbowl, beginning with the 1s. After 5 or 10 minutes, the paired 2s enter the fishbowl. After another 5 or 10 minutes, the paired 3s enter the fishbowl. Each pairing answers a different reflection question. Allow time for a preview if desired before opening the Breakout Rooms. A whole-class discussion following the fishbowls is also an option.

9. Topic Rooms

Assigning specific topics to each Breakout Room allows students the autonomy to explore the topic of their choice. It also allows a specific, focused conversation on a single topic, which promotes a deeper dive into class concepts and encourages more extensive critical thinking. Each topic room can be set up as a work station, with differing topics and activities for students to explore.

Students can be asked to answer specific questions, explore materials, solve problems, or develop their own questions. Students could also make their topic selection the day/week before and email the instructor so the instructor could set up the rooms ahead of time.

There may need to be multiple Breakout Rooms on the same topic, or sub-topic rooms, to ensure that only three to five students are in each room, allowing more engagement opportunities for each student.

If not selected beforehand, the instructor can ask students to select the topic they are most interested in exploring and to send a private Chat with one word indicating their selection. An alternative, while manually assigning students to rooms, is to ask all students to unmute, and one at a time, as the instructor calls out their name, students respond with which topic they selected. They could also use the Raise Hand feature to indicate their topic choice, raising a hand only when their selected topic is called out by the instructor. They could also use the Rename feature to change their name to the number they selected.

Geology: After the completion of modules on Volcanology, Plate Tectonics, and Earthquakes, assign one of these three topics to each Breakout Room. Depending on the number of students in your class meeting, you may need to further divide the topics into subtopics.

Ask students to return to the textbook pages that address their selected topic. Send three Chats (Volcanology, Plate Tectonics, and Earthquakes) to all students with attached files containing a set of questions for them to explore in each of these topic rooms. Allow 10 to 20 minutes for a single topic discussion, then close the rooms. The instructor can also allow students to return to the main session room to request that the instructor move them to a new topic room. Sample questions might include:

Volcanology

1. What are differences in the mechanisms of these magma sources: convergent margin, divergent margin, and mantle plume?
2. What explains the variations in magma characteristics (viscosity, gas content)?
3. How would you explain these varying types of volcanism: spreading ridge, mantle plume, and subduction zone?
4. What are the key differences between these types of volcanic rocks and deposits: lava, pyroclastic, lahar?
5. What are some of the critical differences between the 1980 eruption at Mount St. Helens and the 1883 eruption at Krakatoa in Indonesia?

Plate Tectonics

1. Which type of plate tectonic boundary is the one currently unlabeled in the handout (Divergent, Convergent, or Transform Plate)?
2. What is the difference between continental and oceanic lithosphere?
3. What are the names and locations of the seven large tectonic plates?
4. What is the relationship of continental drift theory to plate tectonics?
5. What are the key differences between movement of the African and Pacific plates?

Earthquakes

1. What is the relationship between earthquakes and plate tectonics?
2. What is the importance of understanding Richter magnitude and Mercalli intensity?
3. What is the significance of harmonic amplification and liquefaction?
4. What technology is used in Earthquake notification systems?
5. What are some of the critical differences between the earthquake in Sumatra, Indonesia, in 2004 and the 1964 Anchorage, Alaska, earthquake?

Media Studies: After the completion of a module on Media Censorship & Propaganda, assign one of three subtopics to each Breakout Room. Depending on the number of students in the class meeting, you may need to assign the same topic to multiple rooms.

Ask students to review an instructor-prepared handout (10 minutes) with definition of terms and a relevant, short case study that addresses a problem for which they want to suggest solutions: Government Use of Social Media for Propaganda, Facebook's Role in Spreading Propaganda, or Corporate Use of Social Media for Propaganda. Send three Chats with attached handout files. Ask students to review the handout on their preferred topic for 10 minutes (solo) before sending them to their Breakout Room.

Once in their rooms, the students should first elect a spokesperson. They then work together to identify the core problems, then write down potential strategies to address these problems. The solutions can include approaches such as new legislation, media reform, voter education, shareholder pressure, citizen pressure, legal actions, investigative reporting, and so on. In their discussion, they can raise issues of 1) the ideology and purpose of the propaganda campaign, 2) the target audience, 3) the media manipulation techniques, 4) the impact of various techniques, and 5) counterpropaganda, if any.

Allow 20 to 30 minutes for each group to identify core problems and record potential strategies, then close the rooms. Upon return to the main session room, each spokesperson from a room with the same topic can share potential strategies with the entire class, followed by class discussion. Then the spokespeople on the second topic can share, followed by class discussion. Finally, the spokespeople on the third topic can share, followed by class discussion.

Cosmetology: After the completion of a module on Basic Safety and Sanitation, assign one of these three topics to each Breakout Room. Depending on the number of students in the class meeting, you may need to assign the same topic to multiple rooms.

Ask students to review an instructor-prepared handout that addresses a topic about which they want to learn more. Send three Chats with attached files (Correct Techniques for Using Beauty Tools, Maintenance of Work Stations, and Sanitation Laws and Regulations). Ask students to review their handout with others in their Breakout Room and then generate five questions about the practices or policies. Allow 10 to 15 minutes for each group to review and generate questions, and then close the rooms. Upon return to the main session room, the students can post questions, one at a time, to the entire class, and any student who has not yet answered a question can attempt to respond. If their answer is correct, the class moves on to the next question on another topic, rotating between the three topics. If their answer is incorrect, another student can attempt to answer, or the instructor can supply the answer or point to the correct source.

TROUBLESHOOTING AND PROBLEM PREVENTION

As soon as you open Breakout Rooms, be sure to monitor to see if students are having any trouble joining the rooms. If they remain in the main session room, ask them to unmute themselves and let you know if they need help joining their Breakout Room. Sometimes they are away from their screen when the rooms are opened, so they may just hear your voice and return to join the Breakout Room without any help. They should have a message that they have been invited to join a breakout room, and they click "Join." If they choose "Later," they can join by clicking the Breakout Rooms option in their Meeting Controls, then "Join Breakout Room."

To help students stay on task, you can Broadcast messages into the rooms (but cannot send Chat from Main Session Room in a Breakout Room). The Broadcast messages can include directions, reminders about timing for switching roles/tasks, or a heads-up when the activity is ending shortly. Click Breakout Rooms in the meeting controls, then Click "Broadcast a message to all," enter the message, and click "Broadcast."

Encourage students to select the "Ask for Help" option (then "Invite Host") if they have questions or concerns while in the Breakout Rooms. The instructor will receive a notification and can join the room by clicking the "Join Breakout Room" option. When anyone is leaving a Breakout Room to return to the Main Session room, they should be sure **not to select the Leave Meeting option**, only the Leave Breakout Room option.

The instructor can let students know that a second option for help is for one student to return to the Main Session room to speak with the instructor and then go back to their Breakout Room with answers for the rest of the group.

REFERENCES

1. Faiella, Filomena & Ricciardi, Maria. (2015). Gamification and learning: A review of issues and research. *Journal of E-Learning and Knowledge Society, 11*, 13–21. doi:10.20368/1971-8829/1072.

2. Freeman, S., Eddy, S. L., McDonough, M., Smith, M. K., Okorafor, N., Jordt, H., et al. (2014). Active learning increases student performance in science, engineering, and mathematics. *Proceedings of the National Academy of Sciences (PNAS), 111*(23), 8410–8415. https://www.scientificamerican.com/article/stop-lecturing-me/.

3. Slusser, Suzanne & Erickson, Rebecca. (2006). Group quizzes: An extension of the collaborative learning process. *Teaching Sociology, 34*, 249–262. doi:10.1177/0092055X0603400304.

4. Walker, M. (2017). *Why we sleep: Unlocking the power of sleep and dreams*. New York: Scribner.

5. Wieman, C. (2014). Stop lecturing me. *Scientific American, 311*(2), 70–71. Retrieved August 2014. doi:10.1038/scientificamerican0814-70.

Main Session Room

MAIN SESSION ROOM

Used effectively, the Main Session Room can be a hub for active learning. Many of the activities established in the room are then conducted through Poll, Chat, and Breakout Room features. There are also numerous Whiteboard activities that can take place in the Main Session Room, but these will be addressed in Chapter 6. This chapter offers learning structures and activities that can engage learners solely inside the Main Session Room. These structures and activities can be used across all disciplines, but as in other chapters, examples are offered through specific disciplines.

Account Settings

For greater security of the class meeting, activate 1) Waiting Room, 2) Require a Passcode, 3) Require passcode for participants joining by phone, and 4) Only authenticated users can join meetings when scheduling new meetings.

I don't recommend that you select either "Start meetings with host video on" or "Start meetings with participant video on" so that instructor and students have time to prepare themselves to turn on their video when ready. I do recommend that you select "Mute participants upon entry" so as to minimize unintended background noises. This can be changed when the instructor is ready and you can allow students to unmute and greet each other. Remind students (using a slide or shared document) to turn up their computer volume if they cannot hear anything.

See Polls and Chat chapters for the appropriate settings in these features.

In the Zoom Fatigue chapter, I recommend not selecting "Sound notification when someone joins or leaves" as it's distracting. I do recommend that instructors select "File transfer: Hosts and participants can send files through the in-meeting chat." I also recommend selecting "Co-host: Allow the host to add co-hosts" if you anticipate other instructor or student tech support during the meeting.

If you want to use Share Screen and Whiteboards, select the following:

- Allow host and participants to share their screen or content during meetings: All participants
- Annotation: Allow host and participants to use annotation tools to add information to shared screens
- Whiteboard: Allow host and participants to share whiteboard during a meeting.

For varied engagement and emotional expression during class meetings, activate "Nonverbal feedback" and "Meeting reactions." I do not "Allow removed participants to rejoin" since they are only removed if they do not belong in the meeting or have seriously violated some norm or class agreement.

I recommend "Allow participants to rename themselves" and do not recommend "Hide participant profile pictures in a meeting." Students can change their Zoom account names to a preferred name, and use the profile pictures for more personalization. These profile pictures can also be leveraged for additional activities (see Chapter 7).

For better audio, I suggest "Allow users to select stereo audio in their client settings," and "Allow users to select original sound in their client settings."

Meeting Controls

The **Security** control feature allows you to modify prior settings such as Share Screen, Chat, Renaming and Unmuting audio. The control feature up arrow next to Mute allows modifications to microphone input and audio output, which sometimes can solve problems for attendees who cannot be heard in the meeting. The control feature up arrow next to Stop Video allows camera options, video setting modifications, and selection of Virtual Backgrounds.

---

1. Strategic Storytelling

Instructors can share short stories with a clear point in order to introduce a topic, provoke interest in the discipline/essential concepts, or demonstrate the value of acquiring new skills. Consider using a related virtual background with the story, and/or starting with a short audio clip.

Bio-Engineering: Share a story about the origins of the hypodermic needle and syringe. Start with some information about an illness that benefited from the development of this medical device. For example, share statistics on deaths or gangrenous limb amputations, or the story of one individual earlier in history with untreated diabetes. Then discuss a few key figures in the development of the hypodermic needle and syringe (showing images if possible), for example:

- The Iraqi/Egyptian surgeon Ammar ibn Ali al-Mawsili developed a syringe in the 9th century from a hollow glass tube to treat cataracts.
- Dating back at least to the 15th century, Native South Americans developed a syringe from sharpened hollow bird bones attached to small animal bladders to inject medicine, irrigate wounds, or even clean ears.
- Irish physician Francis Rynd invented the hollow needle and used it to make the first recorded subcutaneous injections, specifically a sedative to treat neuralgia.
- Alexander Wood, a Scottish surgeon, combined a needle with a syringe to inject morphine into a patient.

Business: Share a few short business start-up stories, then connect them to a lesson on the value of telling a business story in developing a brand. There are many start-up stories, and the instructor can select ones that exemplify the brand development issues in the lesson to follow. The stories should be compelling, right from the start, and represent a wide range of entrepreneurs and business types.

- **Federal Express**, created by 28-year-old Frederick Smith, was the result of Smith's economics paper on improvements in package shipping. Smith, a former Marine pilot in Vietnam, launched the company in 1971, but the company neared bankruptcy within the first three years. Smith's lucky Las Vegas blackjack trip, betting the remainder of company funds, paid off. The company remained in business, and growth has soared ever since. It is currently the world's largest express shipping company.

- **Valence** was founded by Los Angeles–based venture capitalist Kobie Fuller, who found himself inundated by requests from tech companies seeking to diversify their talent pool. Running out of personal contacts to refer, he decided to create an organized network of Black professionals. Along with his co-founders, La Mer Walker and Emily Slade, one of the goals is to solve the problem of Black under-representation in Silicon Valley tech companies, and ultimately to make progress addressing the racial wealth gap in the United States. The company launched in 2019 with $2.5 million from venture capital firms and angel investors.

- **Grameen Bank** founder Muhammad Yunus observed that poor women in Bangladesh could benefit from small loans to help them purchase material to make household items like cooking pots and brooms. The women could then sell those items and use the profits to feed their families. Yet banks would not lend to women in small villages since they had no collateral or credit history. Yunus, using only $27 to start the Grameen Bank, developed the practice of micro-lending. The Grameen Bank has since loaned out over $20 billion to over 50 million borrowers, repayment rates are close to 99%, and 97% of the loans have gone to women in poverty. Yunus was awarded the Nobel Peace Prize in 2006.

Political Science: Before a lesson on the Geneva Conventions, offer a story that demonstrates the importance of these conventions. Let students know that this activity may be disturbing, and then share a story of a victim of a war crime or other violation. Allow time for students to offer their reactions and responses, including their feelings about the atrocity. Then introduce the Geneva Conventions, asking students to identify what protections its adherence might have offered to the victim, what justifications (if any) were offered for its violation, and what consequences resulted.

2. Video Guest

Zoom is an excellent forum to invite a "guest" to the classroom by showing short videos that feature an individual who is having an impact in the field.

After selecting Share Screen, be sure to select Optimize Screen Share for Video Clip and Share Computer Sound (on the bottom left) before selecting the browser window with the video. To avoid broken links, consider downloading the videos in advance and uploading them onto the course management system or other stable site. Be sure they are captioned properly.

Linguistics: To introduce a class on African American English (African American Vernacular English or Black English), show students the TEDx video: The Significance of Linguistic Profiling (https://www.youtube.com/watch?v=GjFtIg-nLAA). Then ask students to 1) Examine the linguistic features, such as syntactical structure, vocabulary, and pronunciation, that are present in African American English, and 2) Respond to Baugh's arguments about linguistic profiling.

Aeronautics: To introduce a class on Propulsion, show students the video: Jacqueline Cochran: Founder of WASPs (https://www.youtube.com/watch?v=9C4_fFQn9-8). Ask students to respond to the arguments about the importance of female pilots, made by Jacqueline Cochran, the first woman to break the sound barrier, who also broke multiple speed, distance, and altitude records. Then ask students to analyze the wing design and GE J79 engine of the Lockheed single engine F-104C Starfighter in which Cochran flew over 1,429 miles per hour, more than twice the speed of sound.

Native American Studies: To introduce a class on Louise Erdrich and Native American Literature, show students the video: Conversation: Louise Erdrich, Author of *The Round House* (https://www.youtube.com/watch?v=sDL5QqH5I1s). Ask students to respond to some of the issues Erdrich discusses in the interview, including violence against Native American women, legal jurisdiction, tribal sovereignty (including the 2020 Supreme Court decision, *Sharp v. Murphy*), character development, and an affinity for print books. Use this class discussion to start an exploration of Erdrich's book, *The Round House*.

3. One-Minute Paper

When students write a one-minute paper, they have an opportunity for introspection, analysis, and/or reflection, all expressed in a concise communication. It can be expanded to two minutes, but the goal of this structure, also called a "quickwrite," is to promote thoughtful consideration while practicing brevity. The complexity of the assignment should be limited to something that could be thoughtfully addressed in only one or two minutes. The one-minute paper can be used as an opening activity, like a pre-instruction prompt, a mid-instruction processing activity, or a post-activity reflection. It's a tool that can be used more than once during a class meeting.

Pre-Instruction Prompts:

Physics: Before instruction on Fluid Mechanics and Newton's law of viscosity: Why does toothpaste only come out of the tube when we squeeze the tube?

Accounting: Before instruction on External, Internal, and Internal Revenue Service (IRS) Audits: How often do audits take place and why are they important?

Human Geography: Before instruction on Migration Patterns: What do you believe to be two major forces leading to significant human migrations?

Any Discipline: What connection(s) can you identify between today's lesson topic and last week's topics?

Mid-Instruction Prompt:

Hospitality Management: In the middle of instruction on Sustainable Tourism: What have you learned about the importance of respecting and preserving the cultures of host communities?

Commercial Electrician: In the middle of instruction on Amperage Levels and Circuit Breaker Boxes: Based on your new understanding of current and circuit breaker function, what single safety recommendation would you make about the use of commercial appliances?

Economics: In the middle of instruction on Personal Finance Economics: Based on your current understanding of the importance of Compound Interest, what investing strategy would you suggest for your own financial future?

Any Discipline: What have you found most/least interesting about our discussion so far? Or. . . When have you felt most engaged during today's lecture? When did you find your attention wandering?

Reflection Prompt:

Spanish: After instruction on Irregular Verb Conjugation: With which verb type can you expect the fewest irregular verbs: *AR*, *ER*, *IR*? Why is this important to know?

Marketing: After instruction on Market Segmentation: If you were developing a marketing campaign to sell a lifestyle app, which of the segmentation categories would you pay most attention to, and why?

- Demographic segmentation
- Psychographic segmentation
- Behavioral segmentation
- Geographic segmentation

Journalism: After instruction on Scientific Journalism: Do you think journalists should take a position on their topic, rather than practice objectivity, as long as they include primary sources in their article?

Any Discipline: If you needed to tell another student what was explored in class today, what would you say?

Feedback Prompt:

Any Discipline: What was the most important main point from today's class?

Any Discipline: What concept is still the least understandable from today's class?

Any Discipline: What could the instructor do to improve your learning in future Zoom classes?

4. Learning Stations

Learning Stations are an opportunity for learners to explore several aspects of a complex topic. The instructor will need to design the stations in advance, organized in modules/folders, and have them available on the course management class site. Each set of station materials should take students about 10 minutes to explore. To engage learners who move through the materials more quickly than average, offer a "Diving Deeper" option at each station. Learning Stations can introduce topics at the start of a lesson or deepen the understanding of more-experienced learners.

Begin by briefly introducing the topic to students, then ask them to visit the CMS for Learning Station 1. Let them know they should view, read, and take notes on the materials in the modules/folders there. They should also write down at least one question, which they will be asked to share when they return. Also let them know that if they finish sooner than 10 minutes, they should open the folder with the Diving Deeper Question. After 9 minutes, make a short announcement that they have 1 minute remaining, and then ask them to return their attention to the main session.

In the main session, in between the learning station visits, use one of several strategies for students to share their learning or questions:

1. Ask students to each send a question through Chat. Select several questions to answer yourself, and pose some of the other questions for students to answer.
2. Ask all students to review their notes, then to write down one valuable takeaway from their learning station (or an answer to a question, if part of the station activity). Call on students, one at a time, to share and explain their takeaway/answer. Ask about one-third of the students in each of the three rounds so that by the end, all of them will have had a chance to share something.
3. In a class discussion, ask students to share their answers to the Diving Deeper Question. Comment and clarify the answers if needed, providing a brief lesson.

Social Psychology: To introduce a class on Attribution Theory, set up the following three stations:

Station 1:

Folder 1: Include a link to the article "Attribution Theory" by Saul McLeod (2012) (https://www.simplypsychology.org/attribution-theory.html).

Folder 2: Diving Deeper Question: Explain the fundamental attribution error.

Station 2:

Folder 1: Include a link to the video "Attribution Theory" by Lauren Reichert (https://www.youtube.com/watch?v=doMOHcTlK7o): 3:06.

Folder 2: Diving Deeper Question: What happens to our motivation to solve a problem when we attribute negative qualities to ourselves as the underlying cause of the problem?

Station 3:

Folder 1: Include a link to the video "Attribution Theory: The mistakes we make" from Blahzinga Psychology (https://www.youtube.com/watch?v=PJgTSgleIb8): 3:11.

Folder 2: Diving Deeper Question: What is the downside of our explaining our behaviors and outcomes using self-serving biases?

Environmental Engineering: To introduce a class on Natural and Engineered Water Systems, set up the following three stations:

Station 1:

Folder 1: Include a link to the video: Clean Water Is Life (https://www.youtube.com/watch?v=ebE1_IOjC70): 5:58.

Folder 2: Include a link to the CDC page on Community Water Treatment: (https://www.cdc.gov/healthywater/drinking/public/water_treatment.html).

Folder 3: Diving Deeper Question: What purification methods do you think were in place in the Kenyan village, if any, prior to the arrival of the engineering team? What purification methods do you think would be appropriate to implement?

Station 2:

Folder 1: Provide a link to the article "Flint Water Crisis," from the Natural Resources Defense Council (https://www.nrdc.org/stories/flint-water-crisis-everything-you-need-know).

Folder 2: Diving Deeper Question: Why do you think the Flint Water Crisis went unaddressed for years?

Station 3:

Folder 1: Provide a link to the article "In the World: A long haul to bring clean water to developing nations," from MIT (http://news.mit.edu/2013/long-haul-to-bring-clean-water-to-developing-nations-1210).

Folder 2: Diving Deeper Question: How would you engineer a solution to the problem of a low flow rate of ceramic filter purification systems?

English Composition: To further explore the topic of writing errors (run-on sentences, comma splices, and sentence fragments):

Station 1:

Folder 1: Include a one-page handout defining and explaining run-on sentence errors.

Folder 2: Include a short one-page sample essay containing five run-on sentence errors. Provide directions that ask students to find and correct the five run-on sentence errors.

Folder 3: Diving Deeper Question: What are the key differences between run-on sentence errors and comma splice errors?

Station 2:

Folder 1: Include a one-page handout defining and explaining comma splice sentence errors.

Folder 2: Include a short, one-page sample essay containing five comma splice errors. Provide directions that ask students to find and correct the five comma splice errors.

Folder 3: Diving Deeper Question: Are you able to use a semicolon to correct comma splice errors? Explain.

Station 3:

Folder 1: Include a one-page handout defining and explaining sentence fragment errors.

Folder 2: Include a short, one-page sample essay containing five sentence fragment errors. Provide directions that ask students to find and correct the five sentence fragment errors.

Folder 3: Diving Deeper Question: What are the differences between phrase fragment and clause fragment errors? Explain and provide examples of each.

5. Scoring Clusters

In this activity, the instructor provides a one-page handout containing information about a key concept or topic (sent as a Chat attached file or uploaded to CMS). Students are asked to read the article, then score their response to a question on a scale from 1 to 3. The instructor then groups the scoring ranges (1s, 2s, and 3s) into three clusters. Each cluster is then assigned a preparation activity, after which members of the different scoring clusters will share their differing perspectives.

The three scores can be set up in numerous ways, for example:

1) Strongly Agree   2) Partially Agree and Partially Disagree   3) Strongly Disagree

1) Yes   2) Maybe   3) No

1) Answer 1   2) Answer 2   3) Answer 3

Chemistry: In a class on Lipid Biosynthesis in plants, provide students with the following statement:

Fatty acid biosynthesis in plants occurs in the cytosol.

1) Strongly Agree   2) Partially Agree and Partially Disagree   3) Strongly Disagree

Ask all the students to do the following: Write an 8- to 10-sentence statement that explains your position on the fatty acid biosynthesis statement. Why do you agree, partially agree, or fully disagree with the statement? Give students 10 minutes to formulate their statement.

Ask students in Cluster 1 to share their statements with the class. This can take place through various modes:

- Sending through Chat
- Reading them out loud
- Posting them in a Discussion Forum in the course management system (CMS)
- Using Padlet to post them on a virtual wall

The 2s and 3s are then invited to disagree and explain why. Ask students in Cluster 3 to share their statements with the class. The 1s and 2s are then invited to disagree and explain why. Ask students in Cluster 2 to share their statements with the class. The 1s and 3s are then invited to disagree and explain why.

Finally, if it hasn't already been made clear, explain that fatty acid biosynthesis in plants occurs in the chloroplasts of green tissue and in the plastids of nonphotosynthetic tissues and not in the cytosol as in the animal cell.

Data Science: In a class on artificial intelligence, machine learning, and deep learning, provide students with the following statement:

The future benefits of artificial intelligence will far outweigh the negative outcomes.

1) Fully Agree   2) Partially Agree and Partially Disagree   3) Fully Disagree

Ask all students to do the following: Write an 8- to 10-sentence statement that explains your position on the artificial intelligence statement. Why do you agree, partially agree, or fully disagree with the statement? Give students 10 minutes to formulate their statement.

Ask students in Cluster 1 to share their statements with the class. This can take place through various modes:

- Sending through Chat
- Reading them out loud
- Posting them in a Discussion Forum in the CMS
- Using Padlet to post them on a virtual wall

The 2s and 3s are then invited to disagree and explain why. Ask students in Cluster 3 to share their statements with the class. The 1s and 2s are then invited to disagree and explain why. Ask students in Cluster 2 to share their statements with the class. The 1s and 3s are then invited to disagree and explain why.

Finally, add any issues for class consideration that haven't already been raised in the discussions, including both positive and negative current uses of artificial intelligence and potential outcomes. Explain related issues like distinctions between machine learning and deep learning, and their intersections, as well as the potential for biased algorithms.

Comparative Literature: In a class on Caribbean Literature, provide students with the following statement:

Exploring his concept of "Nation Language," Barbadian scholar and poet Kamau Brathwaite argues that, "The hurricane does not roar in pentameters." This means which one of the following?

Answer 1: Caribbean poetry has every right to use the imperial languages of its history.

Answer 2: English literary forms fail to capture Caribbean cultural and literary expression.

Answer 3: The Modernist movement did not succeed as a form in Caribbean writing.

Ask the scoring clusters to all do the following: Write an 8- to 10-sentence statement that explains why you selected your answer. Give students 10 minutes to formulate their statement.

Ask students in Cluster 1 to share their statements with the class. This can take place through various modes:

- Sending through Chat
- Reading them out loud
- Posting them in a Discussion Forum in the CMS
- Using Padlet to post them on a virtual wall

The 2s and 3s are then invited to disagree and explain why. Ask students in Cluster 2 to share their statements with the class. The 1s and 3s are then invited to disagree and explain why. Ask students in Cluster 3 to share their statements with the class. The 1s and 2s are then invited to disagree and explain why.

Finally, add any issues for class consideration that haven't already been raised in the discussions, including definitions of Dialect, Creole, Pidgin, and other linguistic and cultural categories. Explain related issues like the Negritude movement, and share the Brathwaite quote from *History of the Voice* (1984):

> "It is *nation language* in the Caribbean that, in fact, largely ignores the pentameter. Nation language is the language which is influenced very strongly by the African model, the African aspect of our New World/Caribbean heritage. English it may be in terms of some of its lexical features. But in its contours, its rhythm and its timbre, its sound explosions, it is not English, even though the words, as you hear them, might be English to a greater or lesser degree."

6. Detective

In this gamified activity, the instructor provides a brief scenario handout and then asks students to discover something important that will deepen their understanding of a key concept or issue. Students are asked to read the brief scenario and attempt to solve the mystery. They receive a set of clues every few minutes that will help them along in their search for an answer.

Any student who solves the problem can send their answer through Private Chat to the instructor (be sure to reset the Chat settings so that only the instructor can receive a chat). The instructor verifies that it is correct or sends them back to attempt to solve the problem again. Provide a Second Case for students who quickly solve the first problem. For the Second Case, increase the complexity and do not send any clues. You might consider awarding Sherlock Holmes, Detective Olivia Benson, Precious Ramotswe (or other) Detective Badges when a student gets the correct answer.

Website Development: Provide students with the following scenario from Stack Overflow (or substitute with another more appropriate to class topics and current technology):

The Php file below renders correctly using Firefox. However, when using Google Chrome, it displays the HTML code instead of rendering it correctly.

```
<?php
session_start();//session is a way to store information (in variables) to be
used across multiple pages.
?>
<!DOCTYPE html>
<html>
<head>
<script src="https://code.jquery.com/jquery-1.12.3.js"></script>
.... //some lines of code
</html>
```

You have 10 minutes to discover the problem and solution.

Possible Clues: What if there were more than one problem?

Are all lines of code in their correct location?

In this instance, one person suggested that placing the DOCTYPE line as the FIRST LINE of the FILE would solve the problem, whereas another argued that session_start must come before any HTML output.

Nursing: Provide students with the following scenario describing Deep Vein Thrombosis:

A patient has the following symptoms:

- Pain, swelling, and tenderness in the calf in only one leg
- Warm skin around the area of the swelling
- Skin turning to a reddish or bluish color over the affected area.

You have 10 minutes to discover the problem and solution.

What do you believe the condition to be?

Based on your finding, if bed rest were required, what is the proper positioning of the patient?

Possible Clues: What might a CT or MRI scan be attempting to locate?

What would the presence of D-Dimer indicate?

Archaeology: Provide students with background information about Stonehenge or the Works of the Old Men found in Jordan, Syria, and Saudi Arabia. Share some of the more recent archaeologist conclusions about Stonehenge being part of a larger sacred landscape of cemeteries, monuments, and shrines and some of the many still unexplained mysteries of their origins and use. Ask them to determine the purpose of its construction, the methods of construction, and the possible meanings of the concentric rings and solstitial alignments. Provide intermittent clues from more recent research conducted by University of Birmingham archaeologist Vincent Gaffney.

For the Works of the Old Men, named by the Bedouin, provide aerial video or Google Earth links for these ancient geolyphs, asking students to determine their function and the purpose of their various shapes. Who might have built them 2,000 years ago? Might the stone landscapes be similar in use to Stonehenge, including their solstitial alignments? Since none have yet been excavated, it makes discerning their origins and function an even greater mystery. Provide intermittent clues from more recent research conducted by Professor David Kennedy from the University of Western Australia.

7. Why, How, What If?

This active learning structure, intended to follow a class lesson, encourages students to sharpen their expertise at developing probing questions. The instructor presents brief (less than 20 minutes) instructor lectures using voice and PowerPoint, punctuated by active learning activities. After the lesson, the students are then asked to develop questions that will deepen the class's understanding of the lesson. The questions are posed to the rest of the class, either through Chat or verbally, which then attempts to answer them.

The questions are of three types: Why, How, and What If. **Why Questions** seek to explore the claims that are being made, to clarify the importance of essential steps in problem solving, and to understand the complexity of a concept or process. **How Questions** attempt to establish reliable sources, define procedural steps, and improve retrieval practice over time. **What-If Questions** are a powerful source of innovative thinking, allow the synthesis of related ideas, and promote conceptual thinking. Examples of Why, How, and What-If questions can be provided to model this process, and the instructor can ask students to attempt to answer them, as well as asking for a reflection afterwards on why such questions are important in developing expertise in a subject.

Mathematics (lesson on calculating area):

Why Question: Why do we need to use Pi to calculate the area of a circle?

How Question: How do you calculate the area of a trapezoid?

What-If Question: What if there were another formula to calculate the area of a rectangle besides Base × Height?

American History (lesson on Civil Rights Movements):

Why Question: Why did the Student Nonviolent Coordinating Committee rely on nonviolent direct action as its strategic approach?

How Question: How did the American Indian Movement frame its legal arguments for the occupation of Alcatraz Island?

What-If Question: What would have resulted if Martin Luther King. Jr., had remained alive to lead the Poor People's Campaign over the next several decades?

Carpentry (lesson on framing walls):

Why Question: Why do most building codes require studs placed 16 inches on center?

How Question: How do you calculate header lengths when using two side trimmers?

What-If Question: What if there were a faster method than snapping chalk lines to lay out walls and set plates?

Student Success/FYE (lesson on Self-Management):

Why Question: Why do many students hesitate to ask for help when they are falling behind in their course assignments?

How Question: How can you use a reminder app to help you be more successful?

What-If Question: What if you were to create a self-management app— what would it do to help you stay organized?

8. Paradigm Shift

Looking to get your students rapidly engaged? Maybe blow their minds! A "paradigm shift," proposed by Thomas Kuhn (2012), is a major change in a previously accepted theory or perspective. Paradigm shifts allow learners to reframe their understanding of critical concepts. They result in students modifying their prior understanding of events, their fundamental knowledge base, or their beliefs about human capacity. Cognitive neuroscience tells us that introducing new perspectives before beginning a class activity can increase engagement, encourage deeper thinking, and provoke questions.

This can invigorate the resulting class session and encourage greater interest and participation in class discussions.

U.S. Government: To introduce a lesson on campaign speeches, share with students the Milwaukee speech Teddy Roosevelt gave directly after he was shot in a 1912 assassination attempt. With a bullet from the assassin's Colt revolver still lodged in his chest, he delayed a trip to the hospital. Instead, he insisted on being driven directly to the Milwaukee Auditorium to deliver a campaign speech. "I don't know whether you fully understand that I have just been shot," he told the audience. "I give you my word, I do not care a rap about being shot; not a rap." He spoke for 90 minutes with a bullet lodged in his chest. The 50-page speech he had prepared and stashed in his jacket pocket had helped to deflect the bullet from lodging in his heart or lungs.

Oceanography: To introduce a lesson on ocean currents, select one of the many related mysteries of the ocean, for example "The Bloop." "The Bloop" was recorded in 1997 by the National Oceanic and Atmospheric Administration (NOAA). It was one of the loudest ocean sounds ever recorded, and although there is various speculation as to whether it was ice related, no one is absolutely certain of its source. It occurred in Point Nemo, at a site in the ocean that is farthest away from land, surrounded by over 1,000 miles of ocean in every direction. It is located inside the South Pacific Gyre: a massive rotating current that prevents nutrient-rich water from flowing into the area. Without nutrients, no ocean life can be found there, with the exception of bacteria and miniature crabs living near the volcanic seafloor vents. Have students listen for a minute to the actual "Bloop" recording (https://www.youtube.com/watch?v=OBN56wL35IQ).

Student Success: To introduce a lesson on Peak Performance, and unexpected human capacity, share one or two stories about incredible feats of performance. The feats might be mental or physical. They should demonstrate the point that humans are often capable of greater performance than expected, with the mind deeply involved in carrying humans past their perceived limitations. For example:

> **Wim Hof,** also known as the Iceman, ran a marathon in the Arctic with a temperature of minus 20 degrees Fahrenheit, without a shirt. He holds a world record for staying immersed in ice for 104 minutes. He wore only shorts while he stood outdoors for over an hour at the North Pole. Hof credits his feats to his ability to use his mind to raise

his body temperature using Tummo, a breathing and meditation discipline practiced by Tibetan monks.

Charlotte Heffelmire was a college student from Virginia, home on break. When she went into the garage, she spotted her father stuck under a collapsed pickup truck, which had also caught on fire from spilled gasoline. Though she weighed only 120 pounds, Heffelmire lifted the truck off her father until he could crawl free, then drove the burning truck out of the garage and put out the fire. Under certain conditions, our minds can elicit unbelievable performance from our bodies.

As posited by Dr. Eric Haseltine in *Psychology Today*, "The remarkable activity in her muscles and adrenal glands had to have started inside her brain, which somehow found a way to command her muscles, along with her adrenal glands, to put forth maximum effort. So, in a very real sense, her life-saving feat was a potent example of what the mind can do when it wants to" (November 6, 2018).

9. Column A, Column B

Motivation researcher Edward Deci has established that intrinsic rather than extrinsic learner motivation is most likely to have a positive impact on learner persistence. One of the major intrinsic motivators is the experience of autonomy. Psychologist William Glasser's Choice Theory defines freedom/autonomy as one of our fundamental psychological needs. All of us, including our students, have a desire to direct our own life and choices.

This learning structure leverages autonomy to motivate greater student participation. The instructor simply offers the class a voice in selecting their next learning topic or task. Create Polls to ask students to vote on their preferred direction when you offer them options. The instructor still has autonomy in designing and leading pathways for students to reach the measurable student learning outcomes for the course, and the students also experience autonomy in making choices at various branches in the class term.

Latin American Literature: For a class that will explore 20th century literature, ask students if they want to dive into magic realism or poetry. If they select magic realism, which of these two authors' work do they wish to explore first: Gabriel García Márquez or Isabel Allende? If they select poetry, which of these two authors' work do they wish to explore first: Julia de Burgos or Isabel Allende? The instructor will still have the opportunity to explore the other authors, but the students are experiencing autonomy in selecting their priorities and their pathway through the course.

Plumbing: For a class that needs to address sanitary systems and plumbing codes, ask students which of the following lessons they'd like first:

1. the components of a sanitary sewer system,
2. the sanitation code of rules and regulations imposed by cities, counties, or states that govern the installation process, or
3. how to correctly install a sewer lateral: trenching, ensuring proper slope, connecting to the city main, and backfilling the trench.

Psychology: For a class on the Science of Happiness, ask students which of the following quizzes they'd like to take:

1. Social Relations and Happiness
2. Gratitude Practices and Happiness

Any Discipline: For any class, ask students which of the following activities they'd like to do next:

1. A paired practice quiz to prepare for the upcoming test
2. An instructor review session using student Chat questions to prepare for the upcoming test

10. Obstacle Race (Hope Theory)

This learner success activity is applicable to **All Disciplines**. The goal of the activity is to encourage students to identify obstacles to academic success, then engage in an activity proven to improve course grades and graduation rates, and to reduce test anxiety.

The activity is based on research conducted by psychologist Charles Snyder, whose research into learner motivation led to the development of the Adult State Hope Scale, which measures Pathway and Agency Thoughts. Pathway Thoughts reference the paths we take to achieve our desired goals along with our perceived ability to create these pathways (Snyder, 2000). Agency Thoughts are defined as the motivation we have to identify and undertake these routes (and required detours) toward our goals. Agency thoughts are based on what we believe about our capacity to improve our lives.

For example:

Pathway Thoughts: Samuel is struggling in his Algebra class. He considers making an appointment at the Learning Center every Monday and Thursday to work with a math tutor. He follows through after class by making an appointment, reminding himself that asking for help is a key quality of successful people. He feels certain that he can revise his plan if he doesn't get the desired results.

Agency Thoughts: Samuel is confident that by following through with this plan, he will be able to master the math problems that are currently confusing to him. He reminds himself that getting tutoring in a previous class helped him increase his grade from a D to a B.

College students with higher Hope scores are more likely to persist to graduation than those with lower scores. Higher scores also translate into lower test anxiety. Finally, Hope measurements have been demonstrated to be more accurate predictors of learner performance than test scores, IQ, or prior grades.

Hope scores can be raised through specific practices:

1. Identifying multiple routes to achieve academic goals
2. Visualizing moving past obstacles and accomplishing these goals
3. Reinterpreting obstacles as temporary barriers to be hurdled

In Obstacle Race, the first step is to ask students to each identify one potential obstacle to their success this term. The instructor asks students to submit this obstacle in advance of the class meeting and shares that it will be used to create a list. Students will be randomly assigned to one of the obstacles on the list and then asked to develop alternative pathways to overcome the obstacle.

The instructor creates a Google Sheet of all the obstacles, removing duplicates. Creating a second column, the instructor then assigns each student one obstacle on the list. Depending on the number of removed duplicates, some students may be assigned to the same obstacle. Creating a third column, each obstacle should have room for three alternative pathways to be entered.

The next step during the class meeting is to display the Google Sheet list and ask students to review the obstacles. In the third column, next to their names, students should write several possible alternative pathways to make it past the obstacle.

For example, if the obstacle is no money for purchasing textbooks, possible alternative pathways might be: 1) using the library's textbook loan program, 2) asking if the instructor might have an extra copy to borrow, or

3) applying for a campus work-study position to get more funds to purchase the textbooks.

The last step is a Guided Visualization. The instructor asks all students to turn off their video, close their eyes, and find a comfortable position. Then ask them, in their mind's eye, to imagine themselves walking a pathway through college. Identify each obstacle they encounter along the way (from the list), noting it is only temporary, then ask them to imagine themselves acting on one of the suggested alternative pathways, reading each one out loud, slowly. Guide them through obstacles and alternative pathways, encouraging them to see themselves selecting an alternative pathway to continue making it through college. After helping them guide themselves past the obstacles, ask them to stop and celebrate the end of a semester, or academic year, or their graduation ceremony.

Ask them to open their eyes. Share with students that the consistent practice of visualizing moving past obstacles and accomplishing goals allows students to raise their Hope levels and improves their academic performance. Encourage them to repeat the activity on their own.

REFERENCES

1. Blahzinga Psychology. Attribution theory: The mistakes we make. *YouTube*. https://www.youtube.com/watch?v=PJgTSgleIb8. Accessed August 19, 2020.
2. Brathwaite, Kamau. (1984, January 1). *History of the voice: The development of nation language in Anglophone Caribbean poetry*. Paperback. New Beacon Books.
3. Centers for Disease Control. Community water treatment. https://www.cdc.gov/healthywater/drinking/public/water_treatment.html.
4. Clean water is life. *YouTube*. https://www.youtube.com/watch?v=ebE1_IOjC70.
5. Cochran, J. Founder of WASPs. *YouTube*. https://www.youtube.com/watch?v=9C4_fFQn9-8.
6. Deci, E. L., & Flaste, R. (1995). *Why we do what we do: The dynamics of personal autonomy*. New York: Putnam.
7. Erdrich, L. (2013). *The round house*. New York: Harper Perennial.
8. Glasser, W. (1998). *Choice theory: A new psychology of personal freedom*. New York: Harper.
9. Haseltine, E. *Psychology Today*. https://www.psychologytoday.com/us/articles/201811/7-extraordinary-feats-your-brain-can-perform.
10. https://stackoverflow.com/questions/38502812/html-render-issue-works-in-mozilla-firefox-but-not-on-google-chrome?rq=1. Accessed August 19, 2020.
11. Kuhn, Thomas. (2012, April 30). *The structure of scientific revolutions*. 4th ed. University of Chicago Press.
12. Snyder, C. R. (Ed.). (2000). *Handbook of hope: Theory, measures, and applications*. Academic Press.

Minimizing Zoom Fatigue

CHAPTER 5

MINIMIZING ZOOM FATIGUE

Introduction to Zoom Fatigue

If your experience is anything like mine, since the spring of 2020, we've all been spending endless hours on Zoom or another videoconference platform, such as Microsoft Teams or Google Meet. If you've spent hundreds of hours sitting through a barrage of virtual meetings, and leading multiple virtual class meetings, you are likely very familiar with Zoom fatigue. Many of our students are reporting experiencing Zoom fatigue associated with their synchronous online courses, along with their social use of Zoom.

In this chapter, I share some of the research regarding the underlying causes of Zoom fatigue and methods to minimize it. You will find practical strategies that you can use in any course while teaching in a synchronous distance learning format. These best practices also promote learner engagement and empower distance learners to better negotiate the challenging online learning environment.

Student and Educator Fatigue

Tired of logging into Zoom for endless college meetings? Anxious about getting back onto the Zoom platform for another semester? Exhausted and aching from sitting in your home office chair staring at the screen? Got Zoom fatigue?

Like our students, many of us have already experienced Zoom fatigue from both distance meetings and teaching, and therefore we have some empathy for our students' experiences. Whether using Zoom or another video-conference platform for distance education, the challenges of Zoom fatigue present significant obstacles to effective teaching and learning.

The good news is there are specific causes of Zoom fatigue and specific remedies, but first . . .

If we were in a Zoom workshop right now exploring this topic, I'd start by asking you to take a quick poll to learn more about your experience with Zoom fatigue. We can duplicate the poll here, so choose the statement that most closely describes your experience with Zoom fatigue:

1. I haven't been on Zoom or any other videoconferencing platform.
2. I've been in a few Zoom meetings, but it's not been a problem.
3. I've been in many Zoom meetings for work, and it's getting a bit tiresome.
4. I've been in endless Zoom meetings for work, and I'm over it.
5. I've been in Zoom meetings for work and teaching, and I'm numb at this point.
6. I've been in Zoom meetings all day long for work, teaching, and social visits.
7. I can't count the number of Zoom meetings in the last months, and it's a haze.
8. I'm using Zoom for just about everything, and I am exhausted and overwhelmed.

Perhaps you've been able to avoid or minimize your own Zoom fatigue, or perhaps you're still in the thick of it, but no matter what your poll response, we know that many students have been struggling with synchronous learning platforms. Their frustration, exhaustion, and disengagement have been captured in endless viral memes . . .

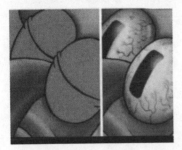

Me sleeping during a zoom lecture and hearing my name being called on

Me with in-person classes

Me with zoom university

Our students often report experiences such as "It's exhausting having to pay attention or go to class, and sometimes I'll have to force myself to pay attention, which is a struggle" (Marco Demelo). Fee Pelz-Sharpe, a 20-year-old college student, raises a common concern about being watched while online, by others or by ourselves: "I think part of it is that I'm not constantly aware of my own appearance in in-person classes, while on Zoom I'm constantly adjusting and readjusting." Another college student, Bernadette Bruu, shares that "everyone is going through the same thing, and that has become part of the fatigue—relatable humor, often from the professor or meeting host, takes up half of the dialogue in Zoom meetings. Fake-laughing through the pain got so old so fast, but it's the only method that professors have embraced so far to counteract how dismal the whole thing is" (Meisenzahl, 2020). **[Gentle note to reader: This book is filled with methods to counteract the "dismal" videoconferencing experience, and I'd like you to consider embracing them so that students like Bernadette have a better learning experience.]**

Many educators, like David Cutler, report mixed feelings: "I feel differently now with having to rely so much on Zoom. I want to help my students as best as I can, but the hours on Zoom are draining, and I struggle to give the best feedback I can. It's definitely taxing, but I don't see any better alternative and I'm grateful for any chance to speak with students during these difficult times, even through video chat" (1). Jodi Eichler-Levine, a religion studies professor at Lehigh University, was so exhausted she "immediately fell asleep" after teaching her Zoom class. "It's almost like you're emoting more because you're just a little box on a screen," Eichler-Levine says. "I'm just so tired" (National Geographic, Sklar, 2020).

L. M. Sacasas, director of the Center for the Study of Ethics and Technology, notes the multimodal challenges attributed to videoconferencing:

Participants are not, in fact, sharing the same physical space, making it difficult to perceive our conversation partners as part of a cohesive perceptive field. They lose their integrity as objects of perception, which is to say they don't appear whole and independent; they appear truncated and as parts of a representation within another object of perception, the screen.

What all of this amounts to, then, is a physically, cognitively, and emotionally taxing experience for many users as our minds undertake the work of making sense of things under such circumstances. We might think of it as a case of ordinarily unconscious processes operating at max capacity to help us make sense of what we're experiencing. (Sacasas, 2020)

The suggested strategies in this chapter address the physical, cognitive, and emotional cost of videoconferencing. Though these challenges do not operate independently of each other, the strategies are organized in this order for the sake of clarity.

---

1. Video Fatigue

As Sacasas suggests, one of the reasons Zoom can be so exhausting is the additional focus needed during video communication to remain attentive to facial expressions, body language, and the subtleties of verbal language. Professor Gianpiero Petriglieri notes that "being on a video call requires more focus than a face-to-face chat. Video chats mean we need to work harder to process non-verbal cues like facial expressions, the tone and pitch of the voice, and body language; paying more attention to these consumes a lot of energy. 'Our minds are together when our bodies feel we're not. That dissonance, which causes people to have conflicting feelings, is exhausting. You cannot relax into the conversation naturally'" (Jiang, 2020).

The dissonance also means that we feel less connected, both to the Zoom meeting and to other people in the meeting, which can also be exhausting. Humans have a deep need for social connection, or a sense of "belongingness," and the failure to experience such connection leads to anxiety, emotional distress, and even long-term negative health consequences (Seppala, Rossomando, & Doty, 2013).

The challenges with connecting also arise because of a lack of synchrony. Jeremy Bailenson, director of Stanford University's Virtual Human Interaction Lab, who is running a study on videoconferencing, notes that research demonstrates that videoconferencing disrupts communication patterns.

Effective communication requires synchrony, or an "interplay of talk, gestures, movement, and timing" between the communicators, according to Bailenson's interview with Betsy Morris, a tech writer at the *Wall Street Journal* (Morris, 2020). This crucial interplay is significantly complicated by audio and video lag, lack of familiar visual cues, difficulty in interpreting multiple faces, and the shift from human interactions in three dimensions to only two dimensions.

Kari Henley, an expert on virtual events, argues that the brain doesn't respond well to the typical video feed offered through a passive Webinar presentation of Zoom learning: "Webinar participants don't see the speaker unless it is a tiny box, don't see each other, and don't feel a part of a group. As a result, we get bored, the brain gets tired, and we start doing other things. Just think about the emails, articles and other websites you personally have perused during a webinar. That is what your audience is doing no matter how valuable the information. It has become a digital Pavlovian bad habit. Our learning and retention go down to the bare minimum and we typically feel very tired afterwards, and our stress responses go up" (Henley, 2020).

In terms of our online behaviors, we're not so different than our students. When our brain experiences threat or overwhelm, and we are under stress, we disengage, then we turn to other experiences we hope will be more positive, or that at least distract us from our discomfort.

Consider your own behaviors in a typical Zoom meeting. Though the information offered may be very valuable, how often do you check email, messages, and social media? Look at the news? Visit Zappos when they're having a sale on shoes? Leave the meeting to make a sandwich? In response to the stresses leading to Zoom fatigue, we often disengage. Our students do the same.

Of course, the less engaged learners are, the less active they are, and the less they can learn and recall later when tested. Thus, minimizing Zoom fatigue of all types goes hand in hand with ensuring higher engagement and better learning, thereby optimizing student success.

Minimizing Video Fatigue

Increase Emotional Intelligence

One method of addressing Zoom fatigue is for students and educators to strengthen their emotional intelligence (EQ). EQ increases our capacity to read and respond to facial cues and experience empathy for others. The greater proficiency we have in this area, the less conscious effort it takes to develop connections with others on an online platform. With increased connection to other learners comes increased focus and engagement. Improved EQ begins with understanding the components of EQ, then using deliberate practice to strengthen our proficiency. Daniel Goleman's book *Emotional Intelligence* (Goleman, 2013) explains the components and specific strategies used in education.

In an article in *Training Journal* by Terence Brake (2017) on virtual emotional intelligence, Brake notes that "Just as in a physical classroom, the virtual facilitator must pay attention to—and manage—emotional dynamics, i.e. they must apply virtual emotional intelligence (VEI). The virtual environment, however, poses additional challenges to the facilitator because of reduced communication and emotional cues."

Use Breakout Rooms

Educators can make extensive use of the Zoom Breakout Room features (see Chapter 3) to address this issue as well. Small-group pairings or trios provide relief from attempts to read facial cues from dozens of participants and allow one to focus on just one or two other people. Both formal Breakout Room assignments with a focused agenda and informal Breakout Room networking breaks can assist in creating a stronger sense of connection and belonging. Students also have an opportunity to focus on the assigned task versus the rapidly shifting images.

Video On

It can be helpful to request that students turn their video on (as often as possible) to allow more frequent viewing of participant facial and other communication clues. When seeing faces, students will usually experience more community than offered by a blank box with only a name. Having video on for the entire class session should not be mandated because students should have the autonomy to take short breaks and to be strategic in what they wish to share of themselves and their lives with the outside world. In addition, the use of video can overwhelm a home WiFi network and lead to frequent dropped connections, so turning video off provides a technological "rest" as well.

You might also ask students to develop a class contract regarding shared behaviors while on Zoom. Often students ask that nobody comment on their appearance or their personal belongings visible in the background. The instructor can post or send through Chat a reminder of the Zoom class contract at the start of each class meeting.

Switch Video Views

As a positive, using Gallery View can allow one to see an entire community of learners. However, the downside is the experience of "visual overload because when we look at a screen, whether it's a computer or a TV screen, our minds are accustomed to processing what is in front of us as a unified whole. But a Zoom meeting in gallery view isn't one unified whole. It's the equivalent of trying to watch 5, 10, 20, or more different TV shows, side-by-side, meanwhile checking a mirror to see how you look. This is incredibly exhausting" (fastcompany). Learners can switch to Speaker View from Gallery View to see a larger image and absorb more expressive cues from the individual speaker (Sanders, 2020).

Turn Away

According to Dr. Christopher Starr, an associate professor of ophthalmology at Weill Cornell Medical College, "Eye strain from hours of screen time can result in eye irritation, dryness, fatigue or blurred vision." Dryness from looking at screen leads to digital eye strain. Our blink rate decreases by nearly 50% when using screens. "When you're not blinking, and you're staring and your eyes are wide open, tears evaporate very quickly," Starr said. "You get dry spots, blurred vision, it can cause redness, pain, and over the course of the day it just worsens and worsens" (Seidman, 2015). Some experts also suggest that for some students on the autism spectrum, the use of videoconferencing might intensify sensory overload triggered by video use, depending on backgrounds, lighting, and images being displayed (National Geographic).

Therefore, it can also be helpful to intermittently (and deliberately) look away from the screen for a few minutes to relieve image sensory overwhelm and eye strain. Students can simply close their eyes every so often, and just listen. They might wish to mute the video, perhaps using a Profile Photo (see Chapter 7). They can look out the window if they're near one, or look at a favorite photo near their workstation. They can look at anything . . . except a constant screen view.

Use 20-20-20

Address eye strain with the 20-20-20 method, recommended by the American Association of Optometry. Turn away from your screen, fixing your gaze at an object 20 feet away, for 20 seconds, every 20 minutes. I suggest you practice this along with your students, perhaps assigning a student timekeeper to remind the class when it's time to use 20-20-20.

2. Audio Fatigue

Not only do we experience video fatigue but we also experience audio Zoom fatigue. Professor Petriglieri argues that "Silence creates a natural rhythm in a real-life conversation. However, when it happens in a video call, you became anxious about the technology" (Jiang, 2020). A recent German study demonstrated that even brief audio delays during conferencing "shaped our views of people negatively: even delays of 1.2 seconds made people perceive the responder as less friendly or focused" (Meisenzahl, 2020). The inevitable sound lags in videoconferencing result in meeting participants forming negative perceptions of the current speaker, whether an instructor or other students. This results in experiences of perceived threat, internal anxiety, lack of community, or simply frustration.

These experiences reduce learner motivation to participate in the class meeting, and the experience of negative emotions such as fear or frustration also undermines synaptic function. We're just not learning well when our cerebral cortex is bypassed for the brain to attend to the perceived threat. Strong negative emotions initiate a stress response. Chronic stress negatively impacts memory and attention span. It takes extra effort to maintain focus on learning under threatening circumstances and produces fatigue.

Research shows that when students sense a possible threat in a learning environment, the result is disengagement and a disruption to cognitive processing. There are delays of audio from weak WiFi connections, distracting sounds from accidental unmuting, and sporadic attempts of multiple participants to speak simultaneously. These audio challenges are another major roadblock to effectively facilitating synchronous learning.

Audio fatigue may not happen with all learners, and the videoconferencing format may improve communication opportunities for some. The University of Québec Outaouais's Claude Normand argues that "People with autism tend to have difficulty understanding when it's their turn to speak in live conversations. That's why the frequent lag between speakers on video calls may actually help some autistic people. 'When you're Zooming online, it's clear whose turn it is to talk,'" Normand says (National Geographic).

Minimizing Audio Fatigue

Use Mute upon Entry and Mute All

In order to reduce auditory distractions, educators can use the Mute upon Entry account setting and the Mute All feature during the meeting to minimize unwanted sounds. You can mute all participants that are already in the meeting as well as new participants joining the meeting.

1. Select Manage Participants.
2. Select Mute All.
3. Select Allow participants to unmute themselves.

You can request that participants unmute if they begin to share but otherwise remain muted. You can also request that students re-mute themselves again after sharing. There are keyboard shortcuts for rapid muting and unmuting:

- Windows: **Alt + A**
- Mac: **Shift + Command + A**

You (and your students) can also enable the use of the SPACE key for a "push to talk" feature. Under Audio Settings in your Zoom client, be sure the box for "Press and hold SPACE key to temporarily unmute yourself" has been checked. This allows a quick push on the SPACE bar to unmute and then immediately resets to mute when the bar is released.

I strongly recommend that you do not select the "Play a sound when participants join and leave the meeting" option, since the constant chimes can be very distracting. Imagine you were stuck for an hour on an elevator that stopped on every floor and on each floor . . . ding, ding, ding. . . .

If you want notification of students entering a class meeting (and greater meeting security), use the Waiting Room feature and the host and co-host will receive a visual notification.

Use the Raise Hand Feature

It may not always be clear whose turn it is to talk. In order to manage the timing of student contributions and avoid simultaneous speakers, the instructor can ask students to click Raise Hand to place the Raise Hand icon beside their name. This simulates a hand raise, and the participant's name will then rise to the top of the Participants List. The instructor can call on the student and ask them to unmute. The instructor can also ask students to raise a physical hand to request a chance to speak. If the instructor doesn't notice the raised hand, the student can send a quick Chat as a backup.

Explore Backup WiFi and Hotspots

Lagging audio is typically a WiFi connection issue. Upgrading your plan for greater WiFi speed is a potential solution, but of course it depends on both availability and expense. It's most essential for the instructor because the meeting host's technology issues impact all the attendees, whereas a single student's technology issues impact only one student (unless they're speaking at the time). Of course, there still exists a digital divide, and not all students will have reliable Internet access at home. The instructor might keep a list of students with unreliable Internet access and check in on them from time to time to ensure that they don't feel forgotten or overlooked, and to offer additional support.

The instructor can also ask attendees to use their cell phone hotspot options (if available) as a backup when their WiFi is lagging and causing sound delays or audio/video freezing. As mentioned earlier, the use of video is the "data hog" in this medium, so turning off video can provide more seamless audio transmission. Participants can also use the Zoom app on their phone instead of a computer if that works to enhance the meeting quality.

Turn to Chat

Another approach to both video and audio Zoom fatigue is the use of the Chat feature, which can bypass an overreliance on video and audio communication by offering another medium for learning and social networking. Review Chat (Chapter 2) for numerous strategies to engage learners through Chat.

3. Physical Fatigue

Working from home be like...

Me: why does my back hurt?
Also me:

Another common challenge is physical Zoom fatigue. If your feet, hips, wrists, back, shoulders, or neck are uncomfortable, you might need to modify your workstation setup and use. But as Alan Hedge, the Director of Human Factors and Ergonomics Research at Cornell University, notes, "If people wait till things start to hurt, already they've waited a little bit too long. . . .If your work-from-home setup isn't ergonomic, you will 'accelerate the onset of musculoskeletal problems ranging from neck, shoulder, back problems, to hand-wrist problems, to leg problems, all because of working in poor postures'" (Torres, 2020).

Physical fatigue can also result from the physical performance required to stay in camera view. "In an in-person meeting, you'd likely shift from side to side, tilt back in your chair, swivel from looking one way to another depending on who is speaking, and lean over to take notes. Unfortunately, in a video call, you're stuck in one place trying to stay in the center of the screen, and moving in any other direction can cause your face to become awkwardly cropped. Furthermore, if you move backward and have a virtual background on Zoom, your face will literally disappear into the ether" (Fastcompany). Hours of staying stuck in the camera view and bypassing natural movement will result in physical discomfort.

Minimizing Physical Fatigue

Proper Workstations

It's the usual advice we've all received many times, but it's too often ignored. Currently the stakes are much higher due to the increased screen hours from the work-at-home situation. Even though instructors may have received information or training on proper workstations, it doesn't mean that our students are aware of these protocols. Many of them have no office workstation at all, and their casual setup multiplied by numerous additional online hours can result in physical discomfort. A classroom filled with students experiencing discomfort leads to less focus and learning, so sharing, modeling, and encouraging best practices in workstation setup are essential. This can include the following:

- Place monitor/screen at eye level to avoid neck strain.
- Place laptop/keyboard at elbow level to avoid neck strain.
- Change laptop location and your position twice hourly—keep moving!
- Seated position should lead to back recline of 15–20 degrees to avoid hip/back pain.
- Keep feet flat on ground or use a footrest to promote leg circulation.
- Keep wrists flat and straight when using a keyboard to avoid tendon strain.

The stakes are also higher because the experience of physical pain, especially as it becomes chronic, diminishes our capacity to learn, reducing cognitive flexibility. We want our students to be operating at peak efficiency in their learning, so it would be great to model our use of methods to diminish physical Zoom fatigue.

Changing Posture

It's important to frequently switch from a seated position to a standing position. Most students will not have a standing desk that can be raised and lowered. A simple workaround is to move the laptop or tablet to a higher location, even on top of a cardboard box or a shelf, especially if they are mostly viewing and not using the keyboard. Many PC monitors also allow for viewing angle adjustments that can allow you to stand and view (and maintain your webcam field). Students can alternate, seated to standing, and the instructor can both model and request this.

Video Off for Energizers

From time to time, students should simply turn off their video and move their bodies. They can stretch, shake, do jumping jacks, run in place, take a brisk walk around the room, or dance wildly. These can be informal and individually determined or designed into the class meeting by the instructor.

Dance Party

I wasn't kidding about the dancing wildly idea. One strategy many of my students seem to appreciate is the Dance Party. First, let students know it's optional, though the research on Zoom fatigue suggests that regular movement can relieve both muscle tension and stress. You can provide them with various options, like turning off the video if they're still perfecting their dance moves and don't wish to be seen. They can dance, stand and just move, march in place, sway side to side, or stay seated but wiggle vigorously. Students with disabilities can move in any way they prefer. From anywhere from one minute to five minutes, you can play audio or a video and invite students to dance.

For the first few parties, you can DJ (and of course you're also modeling getting up and dancing, or your chosen variation). Then I recommend that you allow students to select the music of the day. You should establish criteria for song selections such as 1) The lyrics are not offensive to any in the meeting or outside of the meeting, 2) high energy and super-danceable are best, and 3) songs with lyrics related to a class topic rise to the top of the playlist. Keep the dance party short and sweet, 3–5 minutes or less. Consider offering it in the latter part of the class meeting (a good time to stretch, anyway) so that students motivated by the dance party will stick around and do some learning before the party starts.

I suspect that some educators are skeptical. This is a class, not a party. However, consider the wide body of research (for example, Ryan and

Deci, 2000, Alfie Kohn, 1999, Schmitt and Lahroodi, 2008) that establishes the role that intrinsic motivation plays in human engagement. Intrinsically motivated learners, when encountering desired experiences, are more likely to willingly engage in both learning and retrieval practice. A frequently cited desired experience for learners is . . . fun!

4. Cognitive Fatigue

Working memory has limitations, and when those limitations are exceeded, cognitive overload undermines task completion and memory. Technology distractions increase cognitive load. These distractions include video and audio sensory overload, and attempts at multitasking to manage the increased stimuli. The prefrontal cortex has about four slots of working memory. When asked to attend to more than four tasks simultaneously, our competence at these tasks decreases.

Self-consciousness is also a factor in increasing cognitive load. According to LM Sacasas, during a Zoom meeting, "Thanks to my image on the screen, I'm conscious of myself not only from within but also from without. . . . It would be akin to having a mirror of ourselves that only we could see present whenever we talked with others in person. This, too, amounts to a persistent expenditure of social and cognitive labor as I inadvertently mind my image as well as the images of the other participants."

The extra work of worrying about how we appear, or how we present ourselves to others not only increases cognitive load, but it can also impact social sensitivity and self-esteem. According to research exploring social comparison theory, the common phenomenon of taking selfies and posting them to share your image with others may result in "greater social sensitivity and lower self-esteem of selfietakers" (Shin, Kim, Im, & Chong, 2017). It's like we're all suddenly starring in a reality show broadcast daily, and we've become painfully conscious of our appearance, words, dress, and mannerisms.

Minimizing Cognitive Fatigue

Avoid Multitasking

According to Professor Clifford Nass of Stanford University, "People who are regularly bombarded with several streams of electronic information do not pay attention, control their memory, or switch from one job to another as well as those who prefer to complete one task at a time. People who multitask all the time can't filter out irrelevancy. They can't manage a working memory. They're chronically distracted. They initiate much larger parts of their brain irrelevant to the task at hand. . .The research is almost unanimous, which is very rare in social science, and it says that people who chronically multitask show an enormous range of deficits. They're basically terrible at all sorts of cognitive tasks, including multitasking" (Nass, 2012).

Of course, there are multiple levels of complexity to attend to during learning. However, it's easier to engage in simultaneous related tasks focused on one activity than to switch back and forth doing unrelated tasks. Effective learners attempt only one task at a time. They don't shop online, check Instagram, and message a friend while they're being asked to focus on new learning. An instructor can share some of the basic research on the outcomes of attempted multitasking or ask students to find and share some of their own research. The class can then generate a list of best practices to avoid overloading working memory while in a class meeting.

Practice Focusing

When students are distracted or multi-tasking, they lose focus. According to Daniel Goleman, "The more our focus gets disrupted the worse we do. . . .We learn best with focused attention. As we focus on what we are learning, the brain maps that information on what we already know, making new neural connections. When our mind wanders off, our brain activates a host of brain circuits that chatter about things that have nothing to do with what we're trying to learn. Lacking focus, we store no crisp memory of what we're learning" (Goleman, 2013).

Students can track their level of focus using a rating scale (for example, from 1—What? to 10—I'm right on track and laser focused on this activity). Instructors can use a recurring poll, repeated several times during a class session before or after a learning activity. Rating their focus level offers students an opportunity to understand how often they're losing focus. It also serves as a reminder of the focused attention required during one of the cycles of the learning process. Goleman suggests that "Attention works much like a muscle—use it poorly and it can wither; work it well and it grows. Smart practice can further develop and refine the muscle of our attention" (2013). Practice opportunities can include short breathing and mindfulness activities. An example of mindfulness might be catching ourselves in the act of attempting to multitask, then refocusing back on only the highest priority task.

Use Diffuse Learning Breaks

Beyond focused learning, there is still another cycle to the learning process. In her book *A Mind for Numbers*, researcher Barbara Oakley (2014) discusses the differences between focused learning and diffuse learning.

Focused learning relies on a direct approach to studying and problem solving. The learner focuses attentively on the task at hand. The diffuse learning mode occurs when the learner quits focusing on the learning task and takes a break. They might take a walk, listen to some music, or just do . . . nothing. During this break from focused learning, the brain makes new connections. It's important to alternate between these two modes of learning.

Diffuse learning also engages the parasympathetic system, decreasing respiration and heart rate. It shifts the body from stress to calm. It restores the body from the stress caused by multitasking and cognitive overload. Diffuse learning can serve as an antidote to cognitive Zoom fatigue.

An instructor can build diffuse learning breaks into a class meeting, encouraging students to take authentic breaks in which they are fully walking away from all screens, and letting go of their focused attention on learning a topic or skill. Going outside, if possible, is a great option. After 5 or 10 minutes, the learner can return, ready to use the focused learning approach again.

5. Social-Emotional Fatigue

Social-emotional Zoom fatigue can arise from opposite ends of a videoconferencing experience. On one side, students sometimes experience a lack of connection to other students and to the instructor. Keeley Sorotki, director of knowledge sharing at the Ounce of Prevention Fund, notes that the combination of video lag, audio lag, and unclear conventions on sharing conversation space disrupts our sense of connection to others: "Ask a question and there's silence. You feel like you're talking to empty air" (Morris, 2020).

On the other side, too much connection can also be distressing. The combination of attempting to simultaneously attend to an entire gallery of other learners, set healthy boundaries on a potential video invasion of your home by the entire class, and differentiate the Zoom space for differing work and social activities can lead to far too much "connection" with others. Professor Jeremy Bailenson, director of Stanford University's Virtual Human Interaction Lab, has also found that viewing looming images of other people on large screens can appear "threatening" and reactivates the defensive posture of the sympathetic nervous system (Morris, 2020).

Minimizing Social-Emotional Fatigue

Host Your Event

Virtual events expert Kari Henley argues that "there is an awkward silence at the start of many online meetings while everyone is coming on that is not only wasted time, but it is dangerous time. You are telling your audience from the very start that you really don't matter, so in turn, they barely pay attention" (Henley, 2020). Henley recommends several strategies for creating an integrated online learning environment where meeting attendees feel welcomed and experience greater connection:

- Get on the meeting early and serve as a party host or event MC. Greet them and thank them for attending.
- Request everyone use Gallery View as an opener to see each other.
- Request that everyone unmute and call out a greeting.
- Ask everyone to engage in a short icebreaker activity.

No Shaming (Set Class Expectations)

When I ask students to brainstorm the characteristics of an ideal learning environment, they frequently say these two things: "I want to experience respect" and "I want to feel safe." Instructors can ask students to identify their desired experiences for the course and identify learner behaviors that will both promote and undermine those desired experiences. Earlier in the section on Minimizing Video fatigue, I suggested that it's a good idea to ask students to develop a class contract regarding shared behaviors while on Zoom, and that the instructor can post or send through Chat a reminder of the Zoom class contract at the start of each class meeting. Establishing these expectations and reminding students of their importance contributes to an experience of respect and safety, minimizing distressing emotions like shame or fear that undermine learning.

Set Healthy Boundaries

Zoom has become all-consuming in these days of the Pandemic. One day we will be on the other side (hopefully, by the time you're reading this book), but our work and learning will likely be permanently altered. Managing Zoom fatigue means setting healthy boundaries for videoconferencing use. Everyone should limit videoconferencing meeting time to what's essential and productive and use other modalities for communication and collaboration (remember phone calls?). We can also start to recognize the signs that we are beginning to feel social-emotional Zoom fatigue and be proactive in implementing some of the many tools to address it, including taking breaks as needed or just signing off (the Leave Meeting option is just one click away).

Acknowledge Zoom Fatigue

It might be important for instructors to both acknowledge Zoom fatigue during class meetings and identify the negative emotions that result.

Researchers at UCLA have discovered that "affect labeling" or naming negative emotions diminishes the discomfort caused by those emotions (Lieberman et al., 2006). Instructors can administer polls measuring the intensity of student Zoom fatigue and allow students an opportunity to identify negative emotions that are arising during the meeting. Instructors can set up small-group sessions in Breakout Rooms where students are asked to identify negative emotional experiences from their class meeting and share strategies for managing these feelings. Instructors can also assign students to identify one negative emotion they are experiencing during class and find and share a meme that captures that emotion. Sharing memes helps other students name the discomfort they may be experiencing, and it opens the door for the instructor to implement some additional strategies to address these experiences.

Share Conversation Space

Just like in a face-to-face classroom, there is a risk that some students will share far more than others. Zachary Yorke, a Google User Experience researcher who explores the science of remote communication, notes that "conversations on calls are less dynamic, and the proverbial 'talking stick' gets passed less often" (Yorke, 2020). Instructors can implement numerous strategies to ensure a more equitable conversation space:

1. Ask to hear from students who have not yet shared something.
2. Use Chat and ask everyone to contribute their ideas.
3. Ask for a new spokesperson from each Breakout Room session.

6. All Zoom Fatigue

Given that there's significant overlap between various forms of Zoom fatigue, here are a few overall strategies to consider as well.

Schedule Fewer Meetings

Is every synchronous class meeting necessary? In his book *Death by Meeting*, Patrick Lencioni (2004) argues that most meetings are typically an ineffective use of time. At worst they can be tedious, boring, and unproductive. Meetings should be interactive, not passive, he argues, and they should be clearly structured with specifically defined goals. Perhaps you've experienced meeting fatigue yourself, and for very lengthy meetings, even a growing sense of desperation as the meeting dragged on. This experience, sadly, may be shared by many of our learners.

Instructors might apply the same criteria (structured with specifically defined goals) to class meetings. Rather than holding a meeting because it coincides with a scheduled class time, every meeting should have a clear purpose and intended outcomes. Every meeting should be deeply respectful of the valuable time of the attendees. Instructors might explore the possibility of blending synchronous with asynchronous learning, using synchronous class meetings only when they are well designed, engaging, and have a clear purpose. Additional distance learning can be offered through an asynchronous mode.

Model Best Practices with Transparency

Now that you know more about Zoom fatigue and methods to minimize it, use these methods with your students. Do them yourself, and call them out while you do them, asking meeting participants to try them out with you. Share some of the research on the underlying causes of meeting fatigue so that students have a better understanding of why videoconferencing class meetings are so challenging, and how they can be made better through collaborative efforts.

When you need a break, let students know this, and then actually take a short break. Do the 20-20-20 activity with them to relieve eye strain. Let them know when you're changing your position from seated to standing and invite them to change positions as well. Stop and stretch. Avoid multitasking, and manage your own Zoom fatigue to model this behavior for students.

Use Active Learning Structures

My final recommendation would be to ensure that you consistently use active learning structures as the foundation for your class meetings.

Do not use the Zoom platform to deliver an hour-long lecture using an extended PowerPoint presentation. Lengthy lectures without learner participation are boring and ineffective, and lead to fatigue. Nobel Prize winner Carl Wieman (2014) notes that the "positive impact of active learning on educational outcomes is both large and consistent, decreasing the failure rate in courses and increasing performance on tests. There is overwhelming evidence that the lecture is substantially less effective than active learning." Enough said.

A Word from the Wise

Young people often have simple solutions to complex problems. These may prove useful:

"My brain doesn't feel like thinking today."

–Finn, 4 years old

"Sometimes I fall down on purpose so that I can take a break."

–anonymous 6-year-old

"I'll just take a nap; that's how you solve that."

–Keira, 7 years old

REFERENCES

1. Brake, T. (2017). *Understanding virtual emotional intelligence.* https://www.trainingjournal.com/articles/opinion/understanding-virtual-emotional-intelligence.
2. Goleman, D. (2013). *Focus: The hidden driver of excellence.* New York: Harper.
3. Henley, K. (2020). This is your brain on Zoom. https://medium.com/age-of-awareness.
4. https://bmgator.org/21601/news/teachers-and-students-address-zoom-fatigue/.
5. Jiang, M. [BBC] (2020). *The reason Zoom calls drain your energy.* https://www.bbc.com/worklife/article/20200421-why-zoom-video-chats-are-so-exhausting.
6. Kohn, Alfie. (1999, Sept. 30). *Punished by rewards: Twenty-fifth anniversary edition: The trouble with gold stars, incentive plans, A's, praise, and other bribes.* Mariner Books.
7. Lencioni, P. (2004). *Death by meeting: A leadership fable about solving the most painful problem in business.* San Francisco: Jossey-Bass.
8. Lieberman, M. D., Eisenberger, N. I., Crockett, M. J., Tom, S. M., Pfeifer, J. H., & Way, B. M. (2006). Putting feelings into words: Affect labeling disrupts amygdala activity in response to affective stimuli. *Psychological Science,* 18(5):421–428.

9. Mcisenzahl, M. (2020). What it feels like to experience Zoom burnout and how to avoid it. *Business Insider, June* 20, 2020.

10. Morris, Betsy. (2020, May 27). Why does Zoom exhaust you? Science has an answer. *Wall Street Journal.* https://www.wsj.com/articles/why-does-zoom-exhaust-you-science-has-an-answer-11590600269.

11. Nass, C. (2012). The Man Who Lied to His Laptop: What Machines Teach Us About Human Relationships. *Current.*

12. Oakley, B. (2014). *A mind for numbers.* New York: TarcherPerigee.

13. Ryan, R. M., & Deci, E. L. (2000). Intrinsic and extrinsic motivations: Classic definitions and new directions. *Contemporary Educational Psychology,* 25, 54–67.

14. Sacasas, L. M. (2020, April). A theory of Zoom fatigue. The Convivial Society: Dispatch No. 5. https://theconvivialsociety.substack.com/p/a-theory-of-zoom-fatigue.

15. Sanders, Elizabeth Grace. (2020, April 15). Secrets of the most productive people: I'll be right back: How to protect your energy during Zoom meetings. https://www.fastcompany.com/90490716/ill-be-right-back-how-to-protect-your-energy-during-zoom-meetings.

16. Schmitt, F. F., & Lahroodi, R. (2008). The epistemic value of curiosity. *Educational Theory,* 58(2), 125–149.

17. Seidman, B. (2015). "What too much screen time does to your eyes." *CBS, August* 13, 2015.

18. Seppala, E., Rossomando, T., & Doty, J. R. (2013). Social connection and compassion: Important predictors of health and wellbeing. *Social Research: An International Quarterly,* 80(2), 411–430.

19. Shin, Y., Kim, M., Im, C., & Chong, S. C. (2017). The effect of selfies on self-esteem and social sensitivity. *Personality and Individual Differences,* 111, 139–145.

20. Sklar, Julia. (2020, April 24). National Geographic. https://www.nationalgeographic.com/science/2020/04/coronavirus-zoom-fatigue-is-taxing-the-brain-here-is-why-that-happens/.

21. Torres, Monica. (2020, April 3). This is what happens to your body when you work from home. *Huffington Post.* https://www.huffpost.com/entry/what-happens-body-work-from-home_l_5e84bfb5c5b6a1bb765185df.

22. Wieman, C. (2014). *Large-scale comparison of science teaching methods sends clear message.* https://www.pnas.org/content/pnas/111/23/8319.full.pdf.

23. Yorke, Z. [Google Blog] (2020, April 24). https://www.blog.google/inside-google/working-google/science-why-remote-meetings-dont-feel-same/.

Whiteboards for Sharing

WHITEBOARDS FOR SHARING

The whiteboards and annotation tools offer learners a variety of ways to engage with course materials, create their own materials, and solve problems while receiving feedback. The instructor can assign students to use Share Screen and select Whiteboard to work with the drawing and marking tools or share other materials that students can annotate. The Whiteboards produced by student groups can be saved and shared with others.

Account Settings

Under In Meeting (Basic), enable Annotation. You can also allow saving of shared screens with annotations and restrict annotation to only the user sharing content. Saving shared screens allows both the instructor and all students to review the document's notations at a later time.

Meeting Controls

Click the Share Screen button in the meeting toolbar, then select Whiteboard. The Annotation Tools will be available for use. You can use the page controls in the bottom-right corner of the Whiteboard to create new pages and switch between pages. Only the person who began sharing the Whiteboard has control of creating new pages. When finished, click Stop Share. Remind everyone to be careful in selecting what will be shared from the desktop to ensure privacy.

Annotation Tools

Mouse: Switch from tools to your mouse

Select: Select, move, or resize your annotations

Text: Type comments or key words

Draw: Insert lines, arrows, and shapes

Stamp: Insert stamp icons like question marks or Xs

Spotlight/Arrow: Use a spotlight or arrow to highlight annotations

Eraser: Erase stuff

Format: Format stuff

Undo: Ooops

Redo: Never mind the Ooops

Clear: We're done with this . . .

Save: Save the Whiteboards after concluding the activity

1. Volunteer Scribes (Main and Breakout Sessions)

Just like inviting a volunteer up to the board in a face-to-face classroom, you can request a volunteer to record ideas shared by the class. Ask a student to use Share Screen, selecting Whiteboard, then using Text or Draw to capture responses from the class.

> **Corporate Finance:** In a class addressing the investment principle, the financing principle, and the dividend principle, request a scribe to capture class responses to the following questions:
>
> 1. What are the circumstances under which a dividend is preferable to a stock buyback?
> 2. When not returning cash to shareholders, what types of investments might qualify as meeting the Hurdle Rate, the company's required rate of return?

Anatomy and Physiology: In a class addressing the respiratory system, request a scribe to capture class responses to the following questions:

1. What are the parts of the respiratory system (or mark them as they are identified)?
2. What are the most common diseases of the respiratory system?

Solar Technician: In a class addressing solar installation plans and safety regulations, request a scribe to capture class responses to the following questions:

1. What are the advantages of buying versus leasing options for PV solar installations?
2. What are the OSHA 10 safety regulations that are most relevant to installing rooftop solar PV systems?

2. Solo Problem-Solving with Instructor Feedback

Just like inviting a volunteer up to the board in a face-to-face classroom, you can request a volunteer to solve a problem in front of the class. Ask a student to use Share Screen, selecting Whiteboard, then using the appropriate tools for the problem type. Be sure to remain very positive and appreciative of the students who volunteer to help the rest of the class learn new skills, given that it can be very risky to do a task in front of the entire class and instructor. Using patience and good humor, offer encouragement, feedback, guidance, and support as they attempt to solve the problem. Limit the time for this activity and the time for any one student to 5 to 10 minutes to work on a problem. You can ask for other volunteers to continue the same problem or to begin a new one. This will allow more students to be actively involved.

Dental Hygiene: For a class on periodontics and periodontal disease, ask for a student volunteer to annotate a diagram of the supporting structures of teeth. First have them identify and mark the location for the supporting tissues, periodontium, including the gingiva, alveolar bone, cementum, and the periodontal ligament.

Providing them with additional images as needed, have them solve a problem in identifying any disease that might be present. The patient exhibits swollen, dark red, sensitive, and receding gums. There are pus-filled cysts in the gum tissue, some tooth decay, loose teeth, gaps between the teeth, and exposed tooth roots.

If they believe that there are signs of periodontal disease, ask them to spotlight or highlight the areas or issues and connect them to any one of the four stages:

1. Gingivitis
2. Slight Periodontal Disease
3. Moderate Periodontal Disease
4. Advanced Periodontal Disease

Finally, if needed, ask them to show where (and how) any treatment for periodontitis would take place.

Music: For a class on Reading Sheet Music, ask for a student volunteer to annotate a page of sheet music. First, have them identify and highlight elements of the staff, the clefs, and the notes. For notes, they should also highlight and identify the note head, the stem, and the flag.

They can also identify quarter notes, half notes, whole notes, time signature, and tempo. Finally, they can be asked to play or sing what's on the page.

Research Methods: For a class on using correct American Psychological Association citations in a research paper, ask for student volunteers to annotate a sample page of a research paper, as well as the reference list. Ask them to identify and highlight each area on the sample page that requires an author–date citation, correctly assessing elements such as:

- Treatment of quotes
- Treatment of paraphrased ideas
- Page number references
- Capitalization
- Italics

Then have them review and annotate the reference list, identifying which elements are correct and which need further revision. They should review, among other items:

- Order of elements
- Type of reference
- Capitalization
- Punctuation

3. Drawing Activities

The Draw tool offers 12 different shapes. The Format tool allows changes to line width, font, and text color. Instructors can invite students to draw a collaborative document.

> **Art Therapy:** Request permission (in advance) from a student volunteer (or volunteer yourself) to take the role of a client in an art therapy session. Ask one student to role-play the art therapist, identifying and using one of the many possible approaches: Person-Centered, Cognitive, Behavioral, Gestalt, Narrative, Contemplative Approaches, Dialectical Behavior Therapy, or Mentalization-Based Treatment.
>
> The volunteer client engages in the therapeutic drawing process while being guided by the volunteer art therapist. After 20 minutes of drawing, the therapist asks the client to reflect on the process and look carefully at the drawing, sharing emotional reactions, thoughts, and any meaning they might derive from their drawing.
>
> Afterwards (using appropriate feedback guidelines offered by the instructor), the class can discuss the approach used by the therapist, the session, and the processing that took place at the end of the session.
>
> **Mechanical Engineering:** Assign two students to pair and produce a basic mechanical engineering drawing of a simple machine, perhaps as an introduction to different lines and views. More-advanced and detailed drawings would be done with CAD tools. After they complete their drawing, ask for feedback and questions from other students, then supply feedback yourself.
>
> **World History:** Assign paired students a period of world history to review in advance. In the next class meeting, ask one pair at a time to work together for 10 minutes on a Whiteboard to create a synchronized timeline for their assigned time period that illustrates developments in politics, religion, literature, science and technology, and other areas they wish to include. After their 10 minutes ends, ask for feedback from other students on other elements that might be added. Then ask another pair to create their timeline.

4. Feedback Questions Using Stamp

The Stamp tool offers six different marking options. There are Arrows, Question Marks, Check Marks, Hearts, Stars, and Xs. Instructors can share a document with guiding questions and then invite students to annotate in response. When students stamp Question Marks, for example, it helps the instructor focus their instruction on areas where students may need more help.

Student Success: In a class addressing Fixed and Growth Mindset, create a single-page document that summarizes the characteristics of both mindsets and strategies to shift to a GROWTH MINDSET. Share the document and ask students to use the Stamp tool to annotate the document, in response to the following directions:

"Carefully reading the summary page on Mindsets, use the Stamp tool to make six marks, using only the Question Marks and Check Marks. Stamp a Question Mark wherever the concept is still unclear to you and requires more explanation. Stamp a Check Mark wherever the concept is clear to you and does not require more explanation. You have 10 minutes."

After the 10 minutes end, the instructor can review the annotated page, investing time to further explain concepts (giving examples) that are still unclear to a significant number of students. If there is time, the instructor can also call on students to explain concepts that the majority marked as clearly understood.

Nutrition: In a class addressing Protein Sources in the Diet, create a single-page document that summarizes recent research on the long-term health impacts of red and processed meat consumption. Share the document and ask students to use the Stamp tool to annotate the document in response to the following directions:

"Carefully reading the summary page on red and processed meat consumption, use the Stamp tool to make marks, using only the X Mark. Wherever the summary of research presents a finding that contradicts information from the textbook chapter, or from another source you have read, mark an X. You have 10 minutes."

After the 10 minutes end, the instructor should review the annotated page, exploring the research findings that received the majority of the Xs. Asking students to explain the contradictions and the alternate sources of research, discuss the differing conclusions. Then examine the research studies more closely, exploring issues like bias, industry-funded studies, peer-reviewed publications, meta-analyses, and other relevant issues in research practices.

Genetics: In a class addressing the Genome-Editing Methods, create a single-page document with two different short summaries of how CRISPR works in genome editing. The two summaries should demonstrate two different approaches to explain complex ideas or processes.

Share the document and ask students to use the Stamp tool to annotate the document in response to the following directions:

"Carefully reading the summary page on CRISPR genome editing, use the Stamp tool to make marks, using only the Heart, Arrow, and Star Marks. When finished reading, mark a Heart at the top of the summary that was most clear to you. Then mark an Arrow on the concept that was most clearly explained in your selected summary. Finally, mark a Star on the concept that you feel most confident in being able to explain to someone else. You have 10 minutes."

After the 10 minutes end, the instructor should review the annotated page, asking students why they selected one summary over the other. The instructor can then ask students to explain some of the concepts marked with Arrows. Finally, the instructor can pair students and ask them to use Chat or invite them to Breakout Rooms to explain to their partner the one concept they marked with a Star.

5. Breakout Room Whiteboard Use

Students can use the Whiteboard feature in the Breakout Rooms. Introduce a problem to be solved by the group, or a discussion to be held, give them directions for the activity, and then group them and open the rooms. Ask one of the students to use Share Screen, selecting Whiteboard, then for the group to work together, annotating, highlighting, marking, drawing, and adding text as needed on their board. They can save their whiteboard before returning to the Main Session Room.

> **Triangle Trigonometry:** First create random breakout room groups of three students (larger groups increase activity time and decrease engagement). Provide the following directions to start the activity: "I'm sending you two trigonometry problems in a handout through Chat. When you arrive at your breakout room, one student uses Share Screen and selects a Whiteboard, and then the group can work through the problem together."
>
> Begin with the first right triangle on the handout (where one angle θ is labeled already, as well as the lengths of the sides) by identifying and marking the sides in relation to θ: opposite, adjacent, and hypotenuse.
>
> The sine, cosine, and tangent of θ ($\sin \theta$, $\cos \theta$, and $\tan \theta$) are each defined as a ratio of two sides of the right triangle. Remember the mnemonic from the lesson: SOH, CAH, TOA (Sine is Opposite over Hypotenuse, for example). Write down each of the three ratios, then calculate the decimal values for the fraction. Now apply the same process to the second example.

Provide the following directions before opening the Breakout Rooms: "Everyone should work together to contribute to solving the problem. If your group gets stuck, ask for help from the instructor, using the Ask for Help option. One of you can also leave the Breakout Room to return to the Main Session Room, speak with the instructor, and then can be added back to the Breakout Room by the instructor. Select a spokesperson to present your solution to the class when you return. You will have 20 minutes to solve the problems."

Broadcast a message when there are two minutes remaining, reminding them to also save the Whiteboards, and then close the Breakout Rooms.

Careers and Lifestyles: First create random Breakout Room groups of three to four students (larger groups increase activity time and decrease engagement). Provide the following directions to start the activity: "I'm sending you a Career Readiness activity through Chat. When you arrive at your breakout room, one student should use Share Screen. Select a Whiteboard, draw a line down the middle to create two columns, and the group should then work on the activity together."

Ask one student to give you an example of a Career Readiness competency (like Setting Goals). Then ask them to work together in the Breakout Room to brainstorm at least 12 additional Career Readiness competencies. These competencies should be "soft skills" that improve overall performance rather than "hard skills," like technical knowledge of job-related tasks. For each competency they identify in the left column, they should state in the opposite (right) column why it is an important skill.

Provide the following directions before opening the Breakout Rooms: "Everyone works together to contribute to identifying Career Readiness competencies and why they're valuable. If your group gets stuck, ask for help from the Instructor, using the Ask for Help option. One of you can also leave the Breakout Room to return to the Main Session Room, speak with the instructor, then can be added back to the Breakout Room by the instructor. Select a spokesperson to present your findings to the class when you return. You will have 20 minutes to brainstorm and create a comprehensive list."

Broadcast a message when there are two minutes remaining, reminding them to also save the Whiteboards, and then close the Breakout Rooms.

Sociology: First create random Breakout Room groups of no more than three to four students (larger groups increase activity time and decrease engagement). Provide the following directions to start the activity: "I'm sending you a cross-racial adoption discussion activity through Chat. When you arrive at your Breakout Room, one student should use Share

Screen. Select a Whiteboard, and the group should answer the questions together, recording notes, ideas, responses, and questions on the Whiteboard."

Here are the questions to answer together:

1. What is the definition of cross-racial or transracial adoption?
2. What are the differences between transracial and transcultural adoption?
3. What are your personal experiences (if any) with transracial/transcultural adoption?
4. Under what circumstances do you think children should be adopted by another family?
5. What role do politics, economics, and racial/cultural belief systems play in adoption practices?

Provide the following directions before opening the Breakout Rooms: "Everyone works together to contribute to answering the questions about cross-racial adoption. If your group gets stuck, ask for help from the instructor, using the Ask for Help option. One of you can also leave the Breakout Room to return to the Main Session Room, speak with the instructor, and then can be added back to the Breakout Room by the instructor. Select a spokesperson to present your findings to the class when you return. You will have 20 minutes to brainstorm and create a document with answers to these questions."

Broadcast a message when there are two minutes remaining, reminding them to also save the Whiteboards, and then close the Breakout Rooms.

PREVENTING ISSUES AND TROUBLESHOOTING

Remind students to save the Whiteboards if they are working on them in the Breakout Rooms. It might be helpful to use a poll to have students rate their Breakout Room experience from 1–5 at the end of class (1 = uneven participation to 5 = everyone participated equally) so that the instructor gets feedback and can troubleshoot before the next class meeting. The instructor can visit Breakout Rooms to check on participation and provide encouragement, direction and support as needed.

Virtual Backgrounds
and Profile Photos

VIRTUAL BACKGROUNDS AND PROFILE PHOTOS

Virtual backgrounds and profile photos can be used to introduce variety, reinforce concepts, strengthen memory, offer humor, and establish virtual learning sites. It may be true that some virtual backgrounds and profile photos (especially videos with significant movement) can be distracting, and not all are appropriate for a classroom meeting. However, used strategically, both backgrounds and profiles can motivate learners, increase engagement, and improve learning.

Researchers at the PET Centre at the Clarke Institute of Psychiatry in Toronto conducted research on visual images and human memory. They concluded that "a striking characteristic of human memory is that pictures are remembered better than words. One theory of the mechanism underlying superior picture memory is that pictures automatically engage multiple representations and associations with other knowledge about the world, thus encouraging a more elaborate encoding than occurs with words" (Grady, McIntosh, Rajah, & Craik, 1998).

What about multiple and changing images? The researchers noted that "people can remember more than 2,000 pictures with at least 90% accuracy in recognition tests over a period of several days, even with short presentation times during learning." Thus, the use of images that accompany or reinforce learning activities may prove very useful in enhancing memory, especially if they are directly related to the topics.

Virtual backgrounds can be more rapidly modified than profile photos. They can be changed numerous times during a meeting without needing to log into one's Zoom account. The majority of strategies in this chapter will focus on the use of virtual backgrounds (The application of the recently added Filters feature will be addressed in the next edition). Technical directions for creating and adding lenses, or creating more-sophisticated backgrounds or profiles, is beyond the scope of this book. However, there are numerous online sources that will provide directions for doing so. Making suggestions and providing specific examples of how instructors might use these images during instruction is the focus of this chapter.

There are limitations and technical challenges, of course, in using backgrounds. Not all computers will have operating systems or graphics processors that are current enough to support using a virtual background without a physical green screen in the background. This will lead to ghost images. More tech-savvy instructors and students can help other students problem-solve some of these difficulties, but the instructor needs to be prepared for alternatives if not all students can utilize backgrounds.

Backgrounds may also use more Internet bandwidth, leading to lagging or freezing issues. Ask attendees to close down other applications that use large amounts of bandwidth to improve performance.

Account Settings

Under In Meeting (Basic), activate Virtual Background: Customize your background to keep your environment private from others in a meeting. This can be used with or without a green screen. Also select "Allow use of videos for virtual backgrounds." Do not select "Hide participant profile pictures in a meeting." Turn the Video Filter option on to allow users to apply filters to their videos.

Meeting Controls

During the meeting, to select or change a virtual background, click on the up arrow to the right of Start Video, then Choose Virtual Background. You can select from any backgrounds already in your library or upload a new background. Some backgrounds may require the use of a green screen, and others depend on the operating system version of the computer being used.

Profile Photos

To set up a profile picture in Zoom, launch the Zoom app and click on your name initials at the top-right corner. Select Change My Picture from the menu. You can also do this from your Zoom account.

If you are already in the Zoom meeting, you can right-click on the video preview screen. Choose Add or Edit Profile Picture from the menu. Or click on Participants, find your name in the list of participants, and click on More beside your name. Select Add profile picture.

It can take longer to switch a profile photo, but these can be used for similar purposes as backgrounds. Students do need to have video turned off for the photo to appear. As an example, the instructor can ask students to prepare two alternative photos, "Confused Face" or "Thumbs Up Smiling Face." They can then switch their profile photo to indicate their level of understanding of the lesson they just experienced.

1. Learning Structure

If the current synchronous learning structure is a jigsaw, switch to a jigsaw puzzle or a tool room with a jigsaw. If the structure is the fishbowl, upload a fishbowl (goldfish is optional). When using a Prediction Poll, perhaps upload a brain background or a crystal ball. Be creative in matching the structure to the image, and consider establishing a library of images that are uploaded each time students are learning through that structure. This may help them locate where they are in the learning process and remember the directions for the structure more easily.

2. What's Up Next?

As a visual clue and segue to the upcoming activity, change your background just a minute before the next activity or topic, perhaps leaving it up for a break period in between sessions as well. If the upcoming activity is a brainstorm session, then a stormy background or a massive brain would work well. If it's a debate, two lecterns with microphones and debaters would be a great reminder of the format. This can be a transition background only or be one of the learning structure backgrounds you've already established. If you regularly cycle through the same types of learning activities, uploading a virtual background library into Zoom to quickly signal what's next would be helpful, using the same image each time so that students become familiar with them.

3. Topic Related

Backgrounds can also emphasize the topic being explored at the time. For example, a political science class on Voting and Election Laws can take place at a polling site or in the U.S. Capitol. A Biology class on Cell Division of Eukaryotes can take place while everyone is (virtually) inside of a cell.

For more tech-savvy users, you can also apply lenses and filters to the backgrounds. Snapchat, for example, has filters and lenses that can be used to augment photos and videos. Lenses are augmented reality animation, and filters are static image overlays. These modified images can then be used for Zoom backgrounds and profile photos. Zoom has new filter options as well.

Lenses can be applied using the app Snap Camera (which Snapchat users are familiar with) and choosing the filter. Two recent popular filters for meetings have been potatoes and penguins. I know. You might think it's just plain silly to ask students to turn themselves into penguins, but . . . what if it were a Marine Biology class focused on the 17 varieties of penguins, and each student team presenting on their penguin type also showed up as a different penguin variety?

For students in a Nutrition class making presentations on Root Vegetable Nutrient and Health benefits, it might make complete sense for a student to show up as a potato, or taro, or a yam (I yam what I yam, right?). Also, the visual images research team at Clarke Institute did conclude that increased memory "may be related in part to distinctiveness or novelty, which has been shown to activate medial temporal cortex" (Grady et al., 1998). Offering short lectures to students or asking students to make presentations through the filter of an avatar (animal, vegetable, or mineral) offers distinctiveness and novelty, underscores the topic or central issue, and just might make virtual learning a bit more palatable.

4. Break Reminders

A background displayed during a class break can encourage students to use the break effectively for its intended purpose. If you have asked them to completely check out of screen time during the break, announce the upcoming break while your *Gone Fishin'* sign sits prominently in the background. If you've asked them to take a walk outside, change your background to a sidewalk or trail.

If you've asked them to get up and move around, maybe immerse yourself in a sea of spin enthusiasts or frolicking puppies. If you requested that they stop focusing on direct learning and instead allow the diffuse learning cycle to be engaged, you might change your background to show the slower alpha or theta brain waves that arise during meditation, or even slowly crashing ocean waves.

5. Reflections

When asking learners to periodically reflect on prior content or experiences, you could use a background with reflecting mirrors, sunshine reflecting on the ocean surface, or the sunset reflecting off the glass in tall office buildings. You could be seated next to Rodin's The Thinker, or accompanied by an image of a famous deep thinker: Marie Curie, W.E.B. Du Bois, Albert Einstein, or one of many others. You might choose an image of a figure that is renowned for innovative thought within the discipline you are teaching at the time.

6. Field Trip

Although field trips are possible in a synchronous environment, it takes a lot of planning and creativity. The instructor can be the one who is traveling, either literally or imaginatively. If literally, the instructor's actual background doubles as a new "virtual" background that underscores the learning. For example, an instructor in a Plant Biology class could be on location at a local botanical garden, or in a field close to home.

If it's an imaginative field trip, the instructor can select the background that represents the field location where observation or research is to take place. An Art History class focused on sculpture can take place with the instructor background of the Papua New Guinea Sculpture Garden in California or of the Hirshhorn Museum and Sculpture Garden in Washington, D.C.

7. Energizer or Relaxer

To encourage greater participation during a short activity intended to address physical Zoom fatigue, select an appropriate background. You can use a yoga room for stretching, or a gym for jumping jacks, pushups, or a brief aerobic workout. If you want students to dance, try a club (perhaps with a disco ball), with a crowd and a DJ in the house.

If the activity is intended to relax rather than energize, for example, a mindfulness activity or guided meditation, use a Zen Monastery, a solitary spot on a mountaintop, or a restful location beneath a tree or beside a meandering stream. The stream background could be accompanied by playing an audio clip of running water.

8. Background as Poll

Ask all students to upload two different virtual backgrounds (like a dog and a cat). Rather than using a poll to gather student feedback, ask a question with two options for a response. Then have students respond by changing their background to align with Response A (dog background) or Response B (cat background).

Students can also do something as simple as selecting a green or red background. For example, in a Psychiatric Technician class focused on observing and evaluating new patients with potential anxiety disorders, the instructor could provide a list of symptoms or show a video of a patient interview and then could ask the students to choose one of two possible conditions: Separation Anxiety Disorder (green background), or Social Anxiety Disorder (red background). The instructor can ask students to explain their assessments, alternating between green and red selections.

9. Everyone on Location

For a Fire Science class, have everyone join you at the Training Center or on location at a fire. For Hospitality Management, everyone can be in the same kitchen or at a hotel front desk. For a Nursing class, everyone can be in the simulation and skills lab. For a class on Literature, students can all be on a whaling ship chasing Moby Dick at sea, on stage at an abolitionist rally with Frederick Douglass, or at the Hogwarts School with Harry Potter.

10. Tracking Emotions

Because emotions play a major role in disrupting or enhancing learning, instructors can support the further development of students' emotional intelligence (EQ). One of the components of EQ is the ability to be aware of your emotions while you experience them. Periodically throughout the class meeting, the instructor can request a background selection that represents the current emotion the student is experiencing. The instructor can recommend a library of emotion backgrounds that students can upload to allow rapid selections.

These backgrounds also allow the instructor to be more attentive to learner needs. If there are students who signal that they're feeling "anxious" before an upcoming test, that's the perfect time to share some strategies for reducing text anxiety and scheduling a test review session.

11. Lighten Up

Sometimes it's a good idea just to lighten things up. If you're teaching an Accounting class, you just might want to show up as a calculator every once in a while. For Automotive Mechanics, maybe you show up in your Danica Patrick, Mario Andretti, or Bubba Wallace racing overalls with the Indianapolis Motor Speedway as the background. Some people find Chicken Nugget Face amusing, while vegetarians might prefer Avocado Face. You can Google all these to learn more (or not).

12. Time of Day/Weather

You can use a sunrise background for early morning classes, a sunset for late afternoon, and a starry night background for evening classes. You can also use your background selection to reflect the weather. It's an ideal way to mimic the start of a face-to-face classroom when everyone trudges in on a snowy day and comments on how cold it is, or arrives on a rainy day with their dripping umbrellas.

13. Promoting Office Hours

If you'd like to encourage students to visit your virtual office hours, consider creating a background prominently showing the office hours schedule. Show the schedule in the last few minutes of every class meeting. You can also promote other methods of connecting with students, displaying your social media handles, along with a friendly call to action (Please visit Office Hours today!, or Visit the class Facebook page).

TROUBLESHOOTING AND PROBLEM PREVENTION

Ask all participants to download the most recent version of Zoom to be sure that backgrounds and filters are working correctly and offering the latest features. Direct students to the Zoom Guide addressing Virtual Backgrounds and required OS and other computer specifications for their use.

Ask students who select virtual background videos with distracting movement to find another favorite background.

If not all students can utilize backgrounds, as a workaround, consider asking students to quickly draw a very basic handheld image they can display that replicates a requested background, or print an appropriate online image.

REFERENCE

1. Grady, C. L., McIntosh, A. R., Rajah, M. N., & Craik. F.I.M. (1998). Neural correlates of the episodic encoding of pictures and words. *PNAS 95*(5), 2703–2708.

Integrating Apps

INTEGRATING APPS

There are numerous educational technology apps and many other apps (like productivity apps) that can be leveraged for educational purposes. The point of this chapter is not to list these apps, nor to explore dozens of apps in detail, nor to explain how to use them. The point of this chapter is to share some examples of how two apps, Padlet and Socrative, can be used when teaching through Zoom. If you are already using other apps with your students, the strategies in this chapter can be modified for other apps.

Like Socrative, Kahoot! and Quizizz are excellent and engaging quiz apps, and I recommend them as well. There are quite a few apps, so please use ones with which you are familiar, and which offer the most value for your students. It can take some effort to seamlessly integrate them into the Zoom learning platform, while avoiding additional technology challenges, while also leveraging the Zoom features to support the outside apps.

Zoom has a network of integrated app partners, mainly for the business world. These apps focus on functions such as scheduling meetings, content sharing, logins, marketing, and room collaboration. This chapter does not discuss those apps, which can be found at https://zoom.us/integrations.

There are many reasons you might want to consider using apps while teaching on the Zoom platform. For one, most students enjoy them. For example, when I announce an upcoming quiz, students often sigh, groan, or panic. But when I ask them to join a small group in a Breakout Room and log into their Socrative app for a quiz, they rarely complain, and they often get excited.

It's the same quiz, the same content, but in their preferred technology medium.

Another reason to use apps is to go beyond the limits of the Zoom features. Although polls can be modified for abbreviated quizzing, they are not very effective as a quiz tool. Offering students a wider variety of learning experiences can be helpful in maintaining engagement. Finally, both apps can be used to gamify a course, introducing elements of competition and collaboration, as well as a desired intrinsic motivator: fun.

There are also limitations in using educational technology apps. The typical model is for companies to offer free usage to teachers and students, then as they scale up, to offer premium paid services to underwrite the free accounts. Eventually, they typically downgrade the free services and/or begin to charge for services that were previously free. Even though the premium paid charges can be from $.99 to $9.99 monthly, many educators are unwilling or unable to pay for these apps. Many districts don't underwrite these educational technology apps for their educators.

I don't advocate for any particular app, nor am I compensated for promoting them. I am sharing two apps that I have experience using, that were either free or low priced when I started, and that have a broad applicability to engaging learners.

Account Settings

There are no special account settings that need to be selected to use these two outside apps.

Meeting Controls

Using Share Screen will allow an instructor to display Socrative quizzes while live, as well as to display and review results. It will also allow Padlet walls to be displayed while students are adding or editing items posted there.

Padlet in the Zoom Classroom

Padlet allows users to post on a digital wall, as well as to interact with others' postings. It's similar to asking students in a face-to-face classroom to write sticky notes and then post them on the wall. Users can post messages, images, audio clips, videos, and links to online resources. Sometimes the instructor will want student names to appear on their posts, and other times they might select anonymous posts (which can be approved by the instructor prior to posting). In order to make posts anonymous, deactivate the Padlet setting: Attribution: Display author name above each post?

1. Reinforce Today's Most Important Point/Question

U.S. Government: At the end of a class on Campaign Finance and Elections, before students sign out of the meeting, the instructor asks them to post one of two options: 1) What was the most important main point from this lesson about Campaign Finance Law? 2) What is one burning question you are left with about Public Election Financing after today's lesson? The instructor can use this Padlet to clarify if the intended main points from the lesson were learned. The Padlet can also be displayed through Share Screen to show a set of questions that the instructor answers at the start of the next class meeting.

2. Share Essential Resources

Music: During a class on The Music of the United States, as students are beginning research on the topic of the musical history of New Orleans, the instructor assigns each student a narrow area of focus. The students are given 20 minutes to research their topic. The instructor then asks them to find and post on Padlet an image, video clip, or audio clip that helps to understand 19th or 20th century New Orleans musical traditions. The Padlet is set to show the author's name above the post. Students are then asked to Chat with another student about their posting, allowing them to begin to broaden their understanding of New Orleans musical history. The Padlet can remain published and accessible to students for another week or two as they move deeper into their research paper, providing an archive of useful images, video clips, and audio clips.

3. Strengthen Learning Skills

Chemistry: During a class on Chemical Bonds, the instructor assigns small groups of four students one specific bond type to review and summarize from these choices: Covalent Bonds, Polar Covalent Bonds, Ionic Bonds, and Metallic Bonds. Within the group, different members are asked to find and present information in distinct formats: 1) Images of the Bond, 2) Textual Descriptions, 3) Short Video Explanations, and 4) an Analogy or Metaphor that helps describe the bond (for example: an Ionic Bond is like a bully that wants to grab all your electrons).

Students then post their information on the Padlet. The instructor asks students to use the Padlet to study Chemical Bonds. Rather than studying just one bond, or one bond in only one format, the students are asked to move back and forth between the various formats and bond types, interleaving their studying.

The recent research on learning suggests interleaving (sometimes called varied or mixed practice) is a better learning approach than blocked practice. Blocked practice stays focused on one topic or method only, whereas interleaving mixes together different (but related) topics or forms of practice (Rohrer, Dedrick, & Stershic, 2015).

For example, students preparing for a test can alternate between differing question types and/or areas of focus instead of practicing the same question types repeatedly. In an American History course, they might alternate by studying components of various related historical events rather than a single event in its entirety. Preparation for a math test would include switching between different types of practice problems rather than completing a full set of the same problem types.

Socrative in the Zoom Classroom

This cloud-based student response system allows instructors to develop quizzes, surveys, or competitions to assess student comprehension and keep track of their learning in real time. The students can log into the app on their phone (or use their laptop) and quickly join the quiz room.

The quizzes can be conducted in a wide variety of formats, including the game Space Race, and Exit Ticket, which is used to collect end-of-class feedback. The quiz responses can be multiple choice, true/false, or short answer questions. The instructor can see in real time each student's performance, including their rate of completion, and their percentage of correct answers.

The examples in this chapter focus on individual student Socrative activities in the main session room rather than group activities in the Breakout Rooms, like Chapter 3.

4. Preview Quiz

American History: Before a class on Irish Immigration in the 19th Century, the instructor assigns all students to take a preview quiz and then reviews the answers to start a discussion on Irish immigration patterns, connecting the Irish immigrants' history to students' own family immigration experiences.

The quiz questions can include:

1. If your family immigrated to the United States, do you know when this took place? Y/N
2. If applicable, was your family's immigration voluntary or involuntary? V/I
3. Were the majority of Irish immigrants in the latter period of the 19th century male or female? M/**F**
4. How many Irish arrived in America between 1820 and 1930?

    a. 520,000
    b. 310,000
    c. 9,500,000
    d. 4,500,000 (correct answer)

5. Review Quiz in Space Race

Business: At the start of the class on Financing Small Businesses, the instructor notifies students that there will be a competitive quiz at the end, so they should take notes, which can be used when taking the quiz. Twenty minutes before the end of the class, the instructor assigns all students to take an individual review quiz.

Selecting Socrative's Space Race quiz format, this instructor can start a countdown just before the start of the activity, using Share Screen to show the rockets representing each student's performance ready to blast off. Provide the following directions before beginning the Countdown to quiz time: "I am sending you the link through Chat for a Socrative quiz. Log in to the quiz, enter your name, and use your notes to answer the quiz questions. You will have a total of 10 minutes." Give a verbal reminder when there are 2 minutes remaining (though the quiz should show them time remaining).

In the next 10 minutes, review the answers with students. Spend extra time on the questions where there were more wrong answers. Finally, ask students if their notes were helpful in taking the quiz, and for those who answer yes, have them send a Chat message to all attendees describing their note-taking process. Ask the top three winners of the Space Race to be sure to send their quiz preparation approach, since it resulted in a top score.

Quiz topics are determined by the material addressed by the instructor but could include the following:

- Self-Funding Business Options
- Venture Capital from Investors
- Crowdfunding to Fund Your Business
- Small Business Loans

6. Exit Ticket

Physics: Selecting Socrative's Exit Ticket quiz format, the instructor sets up a short exit quiz. At the end of a class on Electricity and Magnetism, the instructor notifies students that there will be an Exit Ticket to leave the class meeting. Five minutes before the end of the class, the instructor assigns all students to take an Exit Ticket quiz, announcing, "I am sending you the link through Chat for a Socrative Exit Ticket quiz. Log in to the quiz, enter your name, and answer the quiz questions. You will have a total of five minutes. You can leave the class meeting after completing the Exit Ticket."

Potential Exit Ticket Questions

1. T/F: Electricity and magnetism form electromagnetism.
2. T/F: A moving electric charge generates a magnetic field.
3. A magnetic field produces an electric current by which method:

    a. Using a combination of weak and strong nuclear force
    b. Using the Force of Gravity
    c. Inducing Electric Charge Movement
    d. Inducing Electron Movement and North–South Pairing

4. T/F: In an electromagnetic wave, the electric and magnetic fields are perpendicular to one another.
    T/F: I have a medium to high level of confidence in my understanding of today's lesson.

REFERENCE

1. Rohrer, D., Dedrick, R. F., & Stershic, S. (2015). Interleaved practice improves mathematics learning. *Journal of Educational Psychology, 107*(3), 900–908. https://doi.org/10.1037/edu0000001.

Index